THE HOPE OF EPATEEN

by

Maya Gideon

Copyright © 2024 by Maya Gideon. All rights reserved.

This book is a work of fiction. Names, characters, places and incidents are either products of the author's imagination or used fictitiously. Any resemblance to actual events, locales, or persons, living or dead, is entirely coincidental. All rights reserved. No part of this publication can be reproduced or transmitted in any form or by any means, electronic or mechanical, without permission in writing from the author or publisher.

First Electronic Edition: February 2024
First Print Edition: February 2024

I would like to dedicate this book to Chris Hampton for all the help she gave me.

CONTENTS

PROLOGUE
1

CHAPTER 1
How Fun?
3

CHAPTER 2
What Does It Say?
7

CHAPTER 3
Talkie!
11

CHAPTER 4
Green Grass and Goodbyes
15

CHAPTER 5
Uncle Samelle
17

CHAPTER 6
Hope
19

CHAPTER 7
To Berry Berry Hill
21

CHAPTER 8
Some New Friends
25

CHAPTER 9
Vicious Rumors
29

CHAPTER 10
About the War
33

CHAPTER 11
My Birthday
35

CHAPTER 12
A Little Doodle
39

CHAPTER 13
Trouble
43

CHAPTER 14
The Day of the Tragedy
49

CHAPTER 15
The Hero's Reward
55

CHAPTER 16
Gold Stars
59

CHAPTER 17
Welcome the Guest
63

CHAPTER 18
In a Black Dress
67

CHAPTER 19
December Snow
69

CHAPTER 20
The New Year
71

CHAPTER 21
The Beast of February Comes
73

CHAPTER 22
March and Hirram's Birthday
77

CHAPTER 23
New Beginnings
83

CHAPTER 24
The Girl Who Ran Away
87

CHAPTER 25
Two New Best Friends
91

CHAPTER 26
Barn Sleepover
95

CHAPTER 27
The Letter from Hirram
98

CHAPTER 28
July
104

CHAPTER 29
The News
106

CHAPTER 30
The Letter in the Envelope
110

CHAPTER 31
The Secret Meadow
114

CHAPTER 32
When the Sun Sets
118

EPILOGUE
120

NOTE FROM THE AUTHOR
123

ABOUT THE AUTHOR
124

BOOKS BY THE AUTHOR
125

PROLOGUE

    I remember the walk to my one-room schoolhouse. The sun was so bright I had to shield my eyes. It was the last day of school before summer break, so I was in a bit of a hurry.
    I had made my way down to the creek with the little trees around it, which is where I always met up with my best friend, Sophi Nakoni. Sophi was the same age as me – 12.
    Oh, and did I mention, it was our last day of school?!

Maya Gideon

CHAPTER 1
HOW FUN?

"Race you to school, Epateen?" Sophi challenged, jumping over the creek.

We ran as fast as cheetahs hunting their prey.

Reaching the schoolhouse, we rushed in as fast as we could.

"No running in here, girls," Ms. Gelleittay, our teacher, said.

Soon, my friends Eliza Wonony, Hummarra Sineirain, and Kailey Vonnson came in through the old squeaky door.

"Have a seat please, and then we can begin," Ms. Gelleittay instructed.

All of us went to our desks and got settled in.

"Grab your math books. Start on page 104 then stop on page 109," she commanded.

I grabbed my book.

"Listen up! I will let you out early today, but you must do all your work first."

My entire class, me included, shouted with glee.

"Settle down," Ms. Gelleittay said.

So, we did just that, and got to work.

Two hours later, while we were eating our lunch, Eliza asked, "What do you have?"

"My papa made me a sandwich," I answered.

"Well, I got carrots, a sandwich, and blueberries," Sophi said.

Before the war, Sophi and I were rich. After the war, we weren't. But we weren't poor, either.

My family were farmers. Sophi's family owned a shop in town that mostly sold fabrics, but they had other items too. She also had a little brother named Freddrick. He was 7 and very annoying.

After lunch, we went outside for recess. Sophi, Hummarra, Eliza and I played jump rope. Hummarra always won. She was like a deer prancing in the snow. Once we got bored of jump rope, and tired of her winning, we played hopscotch and enjoyed the swings.

Soon, Ms. Gelleittay came outside. "Now, we are going to do something fun!"

"Hmm, I wonder how fun?" Kailey replied.

"Yes, I'm wondering that too," I added. "I don't mean this with any offense, but Ms. Gelleittay isn't really known for fun."

"You all think I'm just a teacher with strict rules and policies, but I must say that, I can guarantee you will all be happy with what you see inside the schoolhouse," she said. "Come along … It'll be fun!"

How fun? I pondered, silently this time, while noticing that, based on the looks of my entire class's faces, they were wondering the same thing.

When we got back inside, there was a wrapped present on each desk.

"A gift for the end of the year," Ms. Gelleittay announced.

We all ran to our desks and opened our gifts.

I got a toy! In 1915, toys were hard to get, so we valued them.

My toy was a brown horse with a black mane. It felt smooth, and it looked so pretty. I couldn't take my eyes off it.

"What did you get?" Sophi asked.

The Hope of Epateen

"Me? I got this!" I showed her the magnificent horse.

"Wow! You got an amazing toy horse there," she said.

Then, she showed me the small glass doll she got. It had stringy hair and a long thin dress. The dress was light pink with green dots on it.

We all proceeded to show each other our presents and thanked Ms. Gelleittay. To our delight, we were then dismissed ... best gift of all!

Sophi and I walked home together ... until we reached the creek.

Its shimmering waters reflected the bold rays the sun gave off. It was a small creek, but the memories and joy we shared there made it feel much larger.

The woods around the creek were peaceful. The only sounds to be heard were the calls of the blue jays and the breeze. The leaves of the trees were now a beautiful and vibrant green, as they were each summer and spring, and in the fall, they were a lovely red, orange, and brown. They blocked the sun from its overly bright light, but not enough to leave the woods in shadows. The woods seemed to always have the perfect lighting.

Sophi headed left into town, and I headed straight home to my farm.

"When's the next time you'll be in town?" Sophi hollered out.

"Why, Saturday, I believe," I answered.

We waved our goodbyes, and I went on my way.

Once I passed the creek and was out of the woods around my farm, it wasn't as sunny. There were a lot of clouds. I approached my house, and my papa was waiting there for me.

"What's ya got there?" Papa asked in his firm voice.

I could tell by the way he was looking at my hand that he was talking about the toy horse.

"Ms. Gelleittay gave it to me," I said, so excited to show him.

"Alright then ... that's lovely. Go start your afternoon chores."

So, I tucked the horse into a pocket on my dress and went to feed my dog, Talkie.

Soon, Papa came up to me. "We have a letter from Nolan."

Maya Gideon

Nolan was my big brother, and he was fighting in the war. I wondered what he had to say in that note. He hadn't sent a note since he left to go fight!

CHAPTER 2
WHAT DOES IT SAY?

My papa opened the letter.
I hoped everything was alright.
As he read the letter, he became motionless. Then, he handed it to me, and walked into the house.
I began to read:

To Papa,

I have missed you and Epateen. Here at the battlefield, I have seen so many things that neither you nor Epateen could imagine. Luckily, I have made many friends. My friend Alexsondryx has been kind to me, but he is greatly ill. I was wondering if you could find medicine that might help. He has the measles. So, Papa, how are you and Epateen doing?

Maya Gideon

From Nolan

P.S. please write back

I decided that I would help my papa write him back. Then, I headed inside to help get supper ready.

After dinner, I got ready for bed and blew out my candle with a *woof*.
I looked at the moon glowing outside my window. It reminded me of when my mother would say I was as pretty as the moon itself. My mother was away, helping as a nurse to war veterans, and she wasn't going to be back for a long while.
I crawled into bed and dreamed of life before the war ... when we were rich, and my mother and brother were home.

In the morning, I went out riding on my brother's horse, Geppeto. We galloped like the wind to town, where we saw the town kids playing marbles. Sophi and another town girl, Annie, were playing against each other. The rest of the town kids had gathered to watch.
"Hi, Sophi! Hi, Annie," I called out as I galloped past.
I pulled on the reins. "Whoa."
I quickly jumped off Geppeto.
By the time I got to where Sophi and Annie were playing marbles, a winner was already decided. All the town kids wanted to play the winner ... Sophi. I couldn't believe it! Sophi was terrible at playing marbles. She lost to everyone in town. How did she win this time?!
That's when I heard her say that her new strategy was really working. *Hmmm*.
I looked at Annie, and she did not look happy. Her eyes seemed to be stuck in an endless stare, and her face was as still as a slab of stone.

"Sophi, you want a rematch?" she asked.
"Nah, I want to play with someone else in town."
Sophi looked at me. "You want to play me?"
Before I could answer, Geppeto ran for the hills. Startled, we all looked to see what he was running from ... and that's when we saw it!

What I witnessed caused me to turn into a statue. I couldn't even blink, and my mouth dropped open.

Some of the kids were running, but I didn't turn around to look. I just couldn't turn away from the horrible scene. I simply stood there ... frozen.

"RUN!" I heard a town kid yell.

Maya Gideon

CHAPTER 3
TALKIE!

All of a sudden, a light-yellow shaggy dog with green eyes and furry short legs came running into the disaster. It was my dog, Talkie!
I called out to him, but he didn't come. So, I began to run, hoping he would follow me.
He soon came running toward me from the bank building with a little boy behind him.
"Come on, Talkie," I coaxed him, but he turned and went back to the bank.
To my horror, he ran into the flames that were now covering the building, shooting out of the roof, and moving onto the next building.
I screamed out his name again.
In what must have been a few seconds but seemed like forever, Mr. Gilleit, the banker, ran out of the inferno with my dog behind him.
"Get out of here!" Mr. Gilleit cried.
"Talkie, come boy, come on now. We've got to go," I said, knowing I was shouting, even though it sounded like more of an echoing whisper.

I ran all the way back to the farm. And while I was running, I looked back a few times to see if Talkie was following me. Every time I checked, there he was, his tongue out, thinking this was a game.

"Papa ... playing marbles ... fire ... Talkie ... ran ... flames," I said, trying to catch my breath.

"Slow down, Epateen ... and then tell me," Papa said.

He stroked my hair like he always did when I was upset or afraid.

I finally caught my breath and was able to spill out the story, "Papa, I went into town to buy the flour you wanted. Sophi and Annie were playing marbles. I decided to watch them. Geppeto ran away, and then we all saw why ... it's a fire! Talkie ran into the flames. Then, he came out safely with a town boy following him. He then ran back in and came out with Mr. Gilleit. So, I ran all the way home, trying to make sure Talkie followed me."

I'm not sure Papa got everything I was telling him as I could still feel my body shaking.

I looked at his face, and I saw his worry.

"No! No! No, it can't be true!" He sputtered.

"Papa, what are we going to do?" I asked in such a soft voice I wasn't sure he could hear me.

"Epateen, get the horses hooked up to the wagon," he said. "Hurry!"

I quickly went over to our horses, Tongo and Breezen. I put the halter on Tongo and led him to the wagon. I attached him to the wagon and then ran as fast as I could to Breezen. Just like Tongo, I put a halter on him and led him to the wagon.

A drop of rain hit his clean white coat.

Tongo looked up at me as I led Breezen to the wagon. His mane was a mess, covered in cockleburs, but his golden coat was shining from the rain.

I soon had Breezen also hooked up.

Papa began packing the wagon.

The Hope of Epateen

The light rain had stopped, and I came back into the moment, remembering the fire. I ran to the creek where I could normally see the sign that said *Bello-Bard Town*.

The town was still on fire, and it had spread. It was covering the roofs of all the buildings as well as the surrounding areas and fields. The rain hadn't been strong enough to put it out. And it was heading our way!

"Papa, we must go now! The fire is close to the Weirret's farm, and it will soon reach us!" I yelled out to my papa, who was now bringing food out to the wagon.

Papa quickly packed the sack of food and said, "Get in the wagon, Epateen."

I jumped in and called Talkie. He ran and jumped into the wagon with us.

Papa got in the driver's seat, slapped the reins, and called out, "Yah! Yah!"

The horses took off.

"Papa, why was there a fire?"

My papa just stared straight ahead and finally said, in a low and very soft voice, "Why, my dear Epateen, I cannot say for sure, but I would not be surprised to hear that we were bombed."

Maya Gideon

CHAPTER 4
GREEN GRASS AND GOODBYES

An hour later, we came to a pond where Geppetto was grazing. He was eating the green clover by the water's edge. He still had on his tack from when I rode him to town.

I hopped off the wagon and fetched him. Then, I led him back to the wagon, where I tied his reins to the hook on the back.

I turned to see what was left of the town, but it was hard to see anything as the flames engulfed it all.

"Goodbye," I whispered.

"Epateen, come on, we gotta keep moving," Papa said, his voice stern.

I got back on the wagon.

"Yah! Yah!"

The horses obeyed my papa's command and began to trot.

It soon turned sunny, and there was not a cloud in sight. I looked at Tongo's golden coat shimmering in the sunlight. Breezen's white mane looked as soft as a cloud and as beautiful as snow.

I looked at my papa's long, dark brown hair, which went down to the end of his neck. Papa didn't have a beard, but there were dark

brown short hairs on his chin. He was wearing his old, rugged shirt that had holes in it and no color, along with his well-worn overalls. Those didn't have holes in them, just some stains. I looked down to see what I was wearing – an old red dress that was fading to more of a shade of rose.
In that strange moment, I decided we had everything we needed.
I yawned and decided to take a nap. I didn't have much room, as most of the wagon was taken by our supplies, but I lay down in the space I had. I covered myself with the blanket Papa had packed for me. It was nothing fancy, just a thick gray blanket.
Soon enough, I closed my eyes and was asleep.

I awoke to my papa nudging me.
"Epateen, wake up. It's dinner time," Papa said, his voice more relaxed.
I opened my eyes, and my papa was standing there with a bowl in his hand.
"I made soup," he said, smiling.
I rose up from my sleeping position and stretched out my arms. Then, I grabbed the bowl. "Thank you, Papa."
He smiled again and went to get himself a bowl.
After I finished my soup, I handed the bowl to Papa and went to feed Talkie. He jumped out of the wagon and quickly started eating.
I looked around. We were now in a forest with big oak trees all around us.
Finished eating, we fed the horses and kept moving.
We were soon out of the forest and onto a prairie. By the time sunset arrived, we had finally made it to another town.

CHAPTER 5
UNCLE SAMELLE

The town was called Bersalin Valley. And it was where my Uncle Samelle lived.

We pulled into fresh grass, then hopped off the wagon and approached the town. We headed up to a house, where Papa knocked on the door.

The door creaked open, and I saw my Uncle Samelle.

"Brother, hello! You here for a reason?" Uncle Samelle asked, a surprised look on his face.

"Our town is on fire," Papa said, hanging his head.

"Oh, I'm so sorry. Please stay here until you're back on your feet. Will you come in?" he asked and motioned us inside his home.

Uncle Samelle was such a kind and caring guy.

After we put the horses in Uncle Samelle's paddock, Papa and I went inside.

"We will not stay here long. We must find a new home. But thank you anyway," Papa said.

"Alright. But stay the night, at least. You and Epateen need rest. I have to run out, but you and Epateen settle in and relax. You need it," Uncle Samelle replied and hugged me.

He then pulled open the squeaky door and stepped outside.

Uncle Samelle's house was not large. The living room had a small wooden table in the middle. In the corner, there was an old chair that was also wooden with a plain burgundy colored covering. There was another chair that looked the same. On the wall was a clock. On the shelf by the clock, there was an antique white lion and a candleholder. Also, there were red roses in a white vase in the middle of the antique lion and the candleholder. Behind us, there was a wooden staircase, which led to an upstairs with a small hallway and three rooms – two on the right side and one on the left side. One room was the restroom. It was simple, not as nice as the one in our farmhouse back in Bello-Bard Town, but it would do. The other room on the right was Uncle Samelle's bedroom. I'd never been in there, but I knew he had a fine-size bed and two shelves with antiques on them. The room on the left side was a guest room. It only had a big white bed in it, but it was a good-size room.

I sat down on the chair closest to the wooden table. Papa sat down on the other chair. We relaxed for a few minutes, and then Papa went to grab our bags.

Not long after, all our bags were in the guest room.

An hour later, Uncle Samelle came back.

"I heard at the grocery store that the fire is out."

"Is everyone safe?" Papa asked, his voice full of worry.

"They said no one died. But there are two injured."

Papa sighed. "I do hope things end up alright for everyone."

"Did you put your bags in the guest room?" Uncle Samelle asked, changing the topic.

"Yes, and thank you for having us staying here," Papa said, his voice soft and still full of concern.

CHAPTER 6
HOPE

That night, we had a feast!

I even got to go into the dining room to eat it, which had a fancy wooden table in the center of the large room. We had turkey and corn.

After we finished eating, Papa told me to go to bed.

I headed up to the guest room where Talkie was, and I fed him right there.

I took off my dress and got into my sleeping outfit. I got into the large bed and suddenly thought, *"Will I ever see Sophi again? And where will we go?"*

Then ... I thought of my mother – her green eyes, her black and silky long hair, her smile that always looked so nice. If she were here, she would tell me that everyone in town would find a nice home and that we would too. She would also say that there was no need for me to worry.

I also thought of my brother. He was still fighting in the war. He didn't know if he would ever come home. And I didn't know if I'd ever see him again, but I did hope I would see him again, and he hoped so too.

But the thing I hoped for most was that the war would end. Of course, it would end, and my brother would come back, and my mother too, and then things could go back to normal.

As I thought about it, though, I realized I was getting older, and I knew my mother would just tell me that we would be okay ... even though it might not be true. I also knew my papa had me go to bed earlier than him and my Uncle Samelle because he didn't want me to hear the truth that they'd be discussing – that we needed to worry, we needed to leave, we needed a home, and we needed hope.

If my mother was here, I thought once more, and I was still a little girl, I would think everything was going to be okay. But, at that moment, I felt hopeless.

I knew that things *could* be okay, but I also knew that *could* was a strong word of only a possibility, not a guarantee. *Who knows where we'll end up?*

At the time, it felt like we were in darkness, with no light, and we couldn't see a thing.

But then, I found the word I needed – *Hope*.

So, I hoped with all I was that we would end up with light and happiness.

"Hope, hope, hope," I whispered to Talkie.

Things were looking bad, but it could change. Couldn't it? I decided not to lose hope, yet.

That is what my mother would do. She wouldn't just say that everything would be okay. She would say that because of the hope she always had. My mother had a lot of hope, and she never let go of it.

If only my father had hope.

Hope is why I kept going, even if my papa was hopeless. Everything was going to be okay, and I didn't just think that, I hoped that ... more than anything.

And I soon fell asleep to the thought of *Hope*.

CHAPTER 7
TO BERRY BERRY HILL

As the first peek of sunlight came through the window and onto my face, my eyes opened.

"Rise and shine," my papa called out from downstairs.

It sounded like he was in a better, happier mood instead of his hopeless, doubt-filled one, which made me happy too.

I got out of bed and put on my blue dress. It was just like the red one, but its color was still shiny.

Talkie wanted out of the guest room, but Uncle Samelle wouldn't like that. He wanted him to stay right there.

I went to the restroom then down the stairs and into the dining room. There, sitting on the table, was a bowl of oatmeal. I sat down and ate it, my papa in the chair next to me. Uncle Samelle was in the chair across from Papa.

"Sleep well, Epateen?" Papa asked.

I nodded.

"We're going to head to Berry Berry Hill today. There is a village there ... the village where your mother is," Papa said, his voice full of joy.

I smiled, sharing in his joy. I hadn't seen her in four months. What a blessing that we'd be with her soon!

After I finished my oatmeal, we put our bags in the wagon. Then, I went upstairs to get Talkie. He was sitting by a window, napping.

"Talkie, Talkie, it's time to head to the wagon."

He lifted his head, then stood up and came right towards me. Tilting his head, he looked like he was talking to me. *Why aren't we home? We are almost always there*, his sweet little face revealed.

"The fire," I answered him.

What are we going to do now? He whimpered.

"I don't know," I replied, "but I am sure it will be alright. We're going to see Mama!"

I knew Talkie probably couldn't understand me, and he couldn't really talk, but he sure looked like he knew what I was saying and believed me.

I opened the guest room door, and Talkie and I ran downstairs. Talkie ran into the dining room, then back into the living room, and jumped up onto the worn-out burgundy chair closest to the small wooden table.

"Epateen, get that dog outside," Uncle Samelle bellowed in his strictest voice.

If you had heard him, at that moment, you would have thought he was mean, but really, he was the nicest guy I knew. Fact was, he didn't allow dogs in his house because he didn't like to clean up the hair they left behind. One time, he had a dog in his house, and he ended up spending an hour of his time just sweeping up the hair.

So, I opened the front door. Talkie ran right out, and so did I. We headed for the wagon, and Talkie hopped right in. I was about to get in, but Papa said, "Go get Tongo and hook him up."

I headed for Uncle Samelle's pastures with Tongo's halter. I put on his halter and then hooked his lead rope onto it, walking him to the wagon and attaching him to it.

We got in and headed for Berry Berry Hill.

The Hope of Epateen

Approximately two hours later, we arrived.
It was called Berry Berry Hill because they grew lots of berries. Its original name was Atinenic Pass.
We went to the hotel where my mother was staying.
My papa went to check in at the front desk.
"Hello, Sir," the front desk worker said.
"I am here to see Anita Vallez," Papa said.
"Who wants to see her?" the man inquired in a polite voice.
"Boone Vallez," my papa replied.
"Alright, we will go get her. She will be here in a minute."
I was so excited that I was finally going to see my mama again! I couldn't help but smile. And it was a great big smile!

Maya Gideon

CHAPTER 8
SOME NEW FRIENDS

I looked at the wall clock. It was 6:30 – my favorite new time of the day … because that's when I saw my mama walking down the scarlet, carpet-covered stairs.

Her face beamed, just like I knew mine was beaming too.

"Mama! Mama! Mama!" I shouted.

Everyone in the hotel's lobby looked at me, but I didn't care. I ran to my mama and gave her a big hug.

A man I didn't know was behind her.

"Epateen, this is Hugh Moddie," Mama said.

Before I could respond, a boy appeared at the side of Mr. Moddie.

"Ah, yes, Epateen, and this is Hirram Caunley," Mama said, placing her hand on the boy. "Epateen, you know I have been working at the Volz's, and Hirram has been helping with their chores."

Mama had gone to Berry Berry Hill because the war had started this town's suffering. It seemed as if there were many people here helping each other.

Papa walked over then gave Mama a big hug and a kiss.

"I missed you both so much," Mama said. "Why are you here, though? Is something wrong?"

Her voice was full of worry.

"Bello-Bard burned down in a fire," Papa replied.

"Oh no! Did everyone get out safely?"

"People are injured, but no deaths," Papa said.

Mama let out a sigh of relief. "Okay, I suppose you can stay at the Volz's too."

"Mama, why are you staying at the Volz's if you are supposedly staying at the hotel?" I asked, so confused.

"Good question, Epateen. Truth be told, tonight is the first night I'll be staying at the Volz's, as they are away visiting their uncle."

Evidently, until tonight, my mama had only been working at the Volz's home, not living there.

Later, we walked down to the Volz's farm. I put Breezen and Tongo in their pasture, with their horse, Pachino. While I was there, I found out Hirram and I had a lot in common. We became friends really fast and started to hang out when we weren't working. There was also another boy there who lived in a cottage near the farm.

One day, a new little boy appeared in the Volz's barn. His skin was the color of coffee, and his hair was all black. He didn't look very old – perhaps around three or four.

"Elvira! Where are you?" someone shouted.

I went out of the barn and saw another boy with brown eyes, coffee-colored skin, and dark black hair.

"Elvira!" the boy shouted.

"Are you looking for the boy in the barn?" I asked and pointed that way.

He ran past me and into the barn. "Oh, Elvira, you shouldn't have wandered off like that."

Soon, he came out of the barn holding the little boy and said, "Sorry about my little brother."

"It's alright. How old is he?" I asked, wanting to start a conversation.

The Hope of Epateen

"Elvira here is three," the boy said.
"Where do you live?" I asked.
"Only like a half a mile away from here," he replied. "Do you live at this farmhouse?"
"No."
"Where do you live then?" he asked.
"Long story," I said, trying to avoid his question. "What's your name?"
"I am Reuben," he said.
"I am Elvira," the three-year-old said and giggled.
"Nice to meet you Reuben and Elvira. I am Epateen," I replied.

From that moment on, we kept talking and, before you knew it, you could say that me and Reuben were friends.

The next day, I introduced Reuben to Hirram.

We all loved animals, loved traveling, and had many other things in common.

I was so happy to have friends again.

Maya Gideon

CHAPTER 9
VICIOUS RUMORS

It was mid-June when I started hearing a lot of rumors. And they were about Mrs. Elker. People were saying she was a witch and that everyone should move away from her. But from what I heard, it sounded like she was just an old lady, who I didn't think was a witch, at all. In fact, one day she was walking by the Volz's with berries, and she was actually really nice.

The boy who started the rumors was Miguel Anthone. He was a couple of years older than me and a big bully, although his friends didn't think so.

One time, I heard Reuben arguing with those boys about Mrs. Elker. I didn't really know the details of the argument, but I knew Reuben's family didn't believe in witches, either.

Later that day, we went over to Reuben's house, and I got to meet his parents. Mrs. Haumphon, his mother, gave us a tour of their tiny cottage. We also met Reuben's little sister, Amelia, who was nine months and three years younger than me. And she sure could sing. She sounded like a bluebird and a nightingale at the same time. I am not sure what she did more though – talk or sing.

Mrs. Elker had been teaching her new songs, so Amelia had been going over to her house. Amelia said she didn't believe in witches either, even though Mrs. Elker had a black cat with green eyes named Haricadah.

We asked her about going to Mrs. Elker's house and what it was like, but we couldn't get a word out of her. Although, we did get a song out of her. And after she finished singing, she told us that she learned that song at Mrs. Elker's.

So, we decided to go over to Mrs. Elker's ourselves.

We knocked on her door and counted to ten, waiting for her to answer.

And when she opened the door, we started thinking that maybe she really was a witch.

She had silky dark brown hair and shimmering brown eyes. Her smile was usually so pleasing, but she wasn't smiling right then. She frowned at us like we were harmful scorpions.

She looked Reuben straight in the eye and said, "Oh, it's the pretty nine-year-old's brother."

"Yes, that's me!" Reuben replied, with pride in his voice.

"Why, little Amelia is doing great!" Mrs. Elker said. "So, why are you here with these *other kids*?"

She said *"other kids"* like we were some ugly, slimy slugs. I couldn't believe what she said or how she said it! She had always been so nice to me and Hirram. I didn't know why this time was different.

We stared at her for a long moment and then Reuben finally spoke up, "These are my friends Hirram Caunley and Epateen Vallez."

Mrs. Elker put up a smile, a fake smile. "Come in, Come in."

We walked inside her home, although I don't think any of us wanted to.

A long hallway led to a living room. Against the wall, there sat a piano. There were also three fancy chairs. Right in front of the piano, there was a stool where you would sit to play. To the side of the piano, there was another fancy chair with white fabric and a nice design of roses on it. Another chair in the room was about eight feet from the hall entryway beside the wall. The final chair was eight feet from the other. Both had the same design as the first one. On the ceiling, there was a fancy chandelier with crystals hanging from it. A doorway led to a dining room.

It was such a nice house that anyone would have thought she was rich. You should have seen Reuben's eyes when he saw it.

I gave Reuben a look, and he snapped out of it.

He turned to Mrs. Elker. "This is a nice house, Ma'am."

I suddenly heard a purr. And when I looked down, I saw the famous black cat with snake-green eyes.

I tapped Reuben on the shoulder.

He looked over at me and raised his eyebrows.

"Look, it's Haricadah," I told him.

"Who?" he asked.

"The black cat with the green eyes. Remember?"

"Oh yeah, Haricadah."

"Oh no, Haricadah!" Hirram piped in, his voice raising several octaves.

I forgot that he was scared of cats. *Oh boy!*

"That's it, right there?" he asked, his lip quivering.

"Yep," Reuben said, followed by an ornery grin.

Haricadah went up to Hirram.

"Get him away from me!" he yelled.

"Well, calm down, child," Mrs. Elker said.

"But … it's a cat!"

"Yes, it's just a cat," I mumbled, so only Hirram could hear me.

"Just a cat?! Just a cat?! They are very frightening animals," he said, shaking his head.

"But Haricadah is nice," Reuben said.

"Just pet him. He won't hurt you," I added, trying my best to get Hirram to calm down.

Hirram reached his hand out and touched the cat on its side.

"That wasn't too bad, was it?" I asked.

"No, but I still don't like cats," he responded and shivered.

Haricadah then left the room, more than likely rather offended.

"We should probably head home, Mrs. Elker," Reuben said.

"Oh, but you just got here."

"We'll come back again, Ma'am," Hirram stated.

Mrs. Elker smiled as we headed for the door. We said goodbye to her and made our way back to Reuben's house, where we all decided Mrs. Elker was definitely not a witch.

Two weeks later, the rumors were gone about her, and we started going to her house more often. She became a friend of ours.

Not too long after that, we got another letter from Nolan. I didn't get a chance to read it because of all the vicious rumors circulating again about Mrs. Elker. I was busy trying to clear her name. But just knowing that we got a letter from my brother made things better. It meant it was still possible that he could someday come home.

CHAPTER 10
ABOUT THE WAR

In early July, I started learning more about the war. I read an article that gave me some good information. It said:

> *...The war began in 1914, after the assassination of Archduke Franz Ferdinand of Austria. His death led to the beginning of the war. Archduke Franz Ferdinand was killed in Sarajevo, Bosnia. He and his wife were shot by the Serbian nationalist Gavrilo Princip on June 28, 1914. Archduke Franz Ferdinand was heir to the Austro-Hungarian Empire.*
>
> *The assassination of Franz Ferdinand started a rapidly escalating chain of events: Austria-Hungary, like many countries around the world, blamed the Serbian government*

Maya Gideon

for the attack and hoped to use the incident as the start of the war to end all wars.

On July 5, Kaiser Wilhelm secretly pledged his support, giving Austria-Hungary a so-called carte blanche assurance of Germany's backing in the case of war...

I finished reading the article.
My mama came into the kitchen, where I was and asked, "What's that?"
She looked over the article. "Why are you suddenly so interested in the war?"
"I want to know what's going on," I told her.
She understood.
My birthday was coming up. I would be 13. I thought about my old town, the fire, and how it started. And that's when I knew that, just like my papa mentioned on the horrible day we left in our wagon, we had been bombed.
In the next article, I read that Great Britain was now being bombed. I wanted to go back and see what happened to my old town.
It wasn't too much longer, though, before my family found a nice house that was in a town nearby Hirram's farm. It was a simple house with a main level and an upstairs.

CHAPTER 11
MY BIRTHDAY

It was July 13th, and it was my birthday.
Reuben and Hirram came over that day. They wished me a happy birthday, and they brought me a blanket that Reuben's mom knitted. It said *"Epateen"* on it. Mrs. Elker also came by. And she brought me some berries.
I was very excited that my friends had come for my birthday and even brought me gifts. It was my first birthday at Berry Berry Hill, and I appreciated what Hirram, Reuben, and Mrs. Elker gave me.
"Want to go on a trail ride?" Hirram asked me.
"Yeah, I would love to!"
There were some trails at Berry Berry Hill. Most of them were behind the old barn that was by the hardware store.
We packed our lunches at my house, so we could eat later during the ride. I got Tongo saddled up, and Hirram got his horse, Bianca, tacked up too. I let Reuben ride Breezen.
After we all got the horses ready, we headed for DiAngelo's Trail, which led to a creek. I had been to the creek before, and it reminded me of the one that Sophi and I would meet at in my old town.

Thirty minutes later, we arrived at the creek. The sun was in the middle of the sky, and it was the perfect temperature to be riding.

We dismounted our horses and got out our lunch. We let the horses drink at the creek, while we ate.

In my lunch basket, I found a cupcake. I had not put a cupcake in there. Then, I saw Hirram and Reuben look at me, each with a big smile. And I knew that they had baked the cupcake and put it in my basket. It was really sweet of them! I had no idea they knew how to bake anything.

I took a bite of it and could immediately tell that they had used corn starch instead of flour. *Ugh!* But I tried not to show any disgust on my face, as I sure didn't want them to see that I didn't like it.

After lunch, we rode back to town, all of us loving the pretty scenery of a trail ride. When we got back into town, the sun was going down, and it was a nice, pretty, orange sunset. We rode the horses back to the Volz's farm and untacked them before returning them to their stalls. Hirram and Reuben then left.

I went inside and dinner was already on the table. My mama and papa were at the table, and it looked like they were waiting for me. They had my favorite dinner – steak! It was a special birthday dinner, just for me!

I asked Papa where he got the steak. With the war going on, we had not had steak in a while. He looked at me with a smile but didn't say anything.

After dinner, my parents brought out a carrot cake. They sang happy birthday, cut me a piece of cake, and put it on my plate. They also cut themselves each a piece.

When were done eating the wonderful cake, I offered to help clean up, but my parents said, "That's okay, we got it."

I fed Talkie.

My parents then gave me a box.

"It's your gift from us," Mama said.

I opened the box and inside was a sketchbook. I was thrilled! It was copper-colored leather and had a strap to keep it closed.

The Hope of Epateen

I went up to my room, sketchbook in hand, and got ready for bed. My first birthday at Berry Berry Hill was great! I couldn't have asked for a better one!

Maya Gideon

CHAPTER 12
A LITTLE DOODLE

Five weeks later, school started, and my teacher, Mrs. Longhorn, was super mean. She was very, very strict.

She caught this boy Henry cheating on a math test and put him in detention for one entire month! One time, I didn't turn in my homework (which was five pages long), so she made me stay in for recess and had me write 100 times *"I will turn in my homework"*. And in addition to that, she had me do five extra pages of homework the next week!

One morning at 8 a.m., I realized what time it was, and that school had already started. I hurried downstairs and got my bag together, went back upstairs and got dressed, and rushed to my mama, informing her I was late, while running out the door. I didn't get far before Mama yelled back at me that I had forgotten my lunch. I sped back to the house, grabbed my lunch, and ran all the way to the schoolhouse. I think it was around 8:30 when I got there.

I slammed the door shut, interrupting Mrs. Longhorn. Of course, I was punished for that. She told me I would have detention for the rest of the week.

Maya Gideon

Later that same day, I got really bored during Math. So, I pulled out my sketchbook and started making a few doodles. I drew birds flying above hills, mountains that were very tall, and other random scribbles. When I drew, I was in my own world. I saw birds flying in the great big, blue sky, mountains that could touch the clouds, rivers with bright blue water, woods with fresh green leaves, mythical creatures of all sorts, long hills with cheerful grass, and colorful paths to follow. This was the world that was in my sketchbook – a world that I loved.

But all of a sudden, I was back in the real world ... with Mrs. Longhorn standing right in front of me!

I saw her angry face and quickly shut my sketchbook. I began to put it away, but I was interrupted.

"Stop! I want to see that."

I didn't give her the sketchbook. I kept it closed on my desk.

She raised one eyebrow. "Well? Are you going to let me see that?"

"No," I said softly. *Did I just say that out loud?*

"Give me that!" Mrs. Longhorn yelled.

"No!" I yelled back.

I gripped my sketchbook with all my might.

"Tell me, dear. What did you just say to me?" Mrs. Longhorn said, way too calm.

I knew I had already gotten myself in enough trouble for one day, and that I definitely didn't need to make it worse. "Sorry."

I handed her the sketchbook.

Really, I wasn't sorry, but I also knew this wasn't going to end well for me.

Mrs. Longhorn opened the sketchbook.

She frowned.

"What is this, Epateen?" she asked.

"It's just a little doodle."

"Dear, you should be focusing on your education rather than doodling. Now, I am disappointed in you. You will be put in detention for a month and write fifty times, *"I will not doodle in class"* and also write

The Hope of Epateen

"*I will pay attention in class*" fifty times. You will also stay in during recess. Oh, and I am going to keep this."

When she said she was not giving back my sketchbook, I was *MAD!* My parents worked very hard to get that for me, and I wasn't going to let her take it away.

"Hey! Give me my sketchbook back!" I yelled.

"Settle down. You need to have it taken away. I am just doing my job," she said.

"I'll do everything else, just give that back to me. It means a lot to me," I said, about to cry.

"You should have thought about that before you drew in it while I was teaching," she replied.

Now ... I was *really, REALLY MAD!* And I didn't care about any punishment she could still give me.

I jumped out of my seat and ripped my sketchbook from her hands. I grabbed my bag and began to run out the door.

"That's it! You're suspended!" I heard her yell at the top of her lungs as I ran out the door.

I ran all the way home, relieved I had my sketchbook.

I slammed the door shut and put my sketchbook on the kitchen table. I sat down, taking deep breaths, still shocked about what had happened.

My mom walked into the room. "Why aren't you at school?"

"Umm ... I'd rather not talk about it. Besides, you'll be hearing about it from Mrs. Longhorn."

"What happened?" she asked me again.

"I told you, I don't want to talk about it."

"C'mon. Tell me."

"Fine. I got suspended."

"For being late?"

"No," I said.

"Then why were you suspended?"

"Why do you want to know now? Mrs. Longhorn will inform you," I replied.

"Epateen, what did you do?" my mama asked, evidently not willing to give up until I told her.

"I am not telling you," I said.

I left the kitchen and went to my room.

A little while later, Mama came into my room, and sat on my bed, where I had my head buried beneath my favorite quilt.

She stroked my hair and rubbed my back and said, "It's okay, Epateen, I know what happened, and I'm glad you got your sketchbook back."

My mama is the best!

CHAPTER 13
TROUBLE

Knock-Knock.
I went to answer the door.
It was Reuben and Hirram.
"Do you want to ride down to Dillard's Lake?" they asked.
"As much as I would love to, I can't," I said.
"Why not?" Reuben asked.
"I am grounded for being suspended."
"That's a shame because the new trail is opening up tomorrow. I was thinking we could all go on a ride, but I guess not."
"Oh yeah, right. Duke's Trail is opening up. I can't miss that," I said, trying to come up with a way out of my predicament.
"Looks like you have to," Hirram said and shrugged.
"No, I can sneak out," I said.
"What do you mean?! You can't do that," Reuben said, his eyes so wide they were about to bust out of his head.
"Why not?" I said, thinking I was probably up for the challenge.
"Think about it, Epateen, it's too risky," he said.

"You're right. It is risky," I said and sighed. "But I still can't miss that opening. I have to figure out some way to go."

Later that afternoon, my papa walked into the kitchen after getting home from work.

"Hey, Papa, how was your day?"

"Oh, Pie, it went … it went," he said, with a rather strange and faraway look in his eyes.

"Was it good? Or bad?" I continued to question him, already knowing it wasn't great because he called me Pie, which he only did when he was feeling down and hopeless.

"Oh … well … it went okay," he finally said. "And you? How was your day?"

"Well, I didn't hang out with my friends, if that's what you mean," I said, trying not to be too snooty.

"Okay, well in case you were wondering, that is not what I meant," he said.

"Sorry, Papa, I wasn't trying to be rude. I'm just a little upset that I'm grounded."

"Kiddo, I know this must be hard for you, worrying every day about your brother, hearing your mama and I talk about the war and how scared we are for Nolan. Then, I suppose, being grounded doesn't help. You also won't be going to school this week, so there's that. I'm sorry about all that's going on," he said, and I could tell he meant it.

Something hit me, though, when he said the part about Nolan. I actually hadn't thought about him in a long while. And I missed him.

"Ah … yeah, yeah. Could you do something for me?" I asked, so hoping he would.

Papa raised one eyebrow. "What would that be?"

"Umm … well … Duke's Trail opens up tomorrow – " I didn't finish.

"You want to go," Papa finished for me.

I nodded my head.

The Hope of Epateen

My papa nodded his head. "You want me to unground you."

I didn't answer, not sure what was the best thing to say.

"I think you should talk to your mama before turning to me. I mean, it was she who grounded you," he said, followed by a weary smile.

"Papa, please!" I begged.

"Hon, you need to talk to your mama," he said and left the room.

I knew I wasn't going to get ungrounded by Mama, and my papa wasn't going to get that accomplished either. But I had to go to that trail opening!

The thought of sneaking out came back to me, but I knew that wouldn't work. So, I had to come up with another way.

I grabbed my toy horse that I got from my old teacher the week of the fire. I felt its smooth texture. Holding it always made me wonder whatever happened to my best friend Sophi Nakoni. She'd know exactly what I needed to do.

My mama suddenly came into the room. "Epateen, I know you are grounded, but could you grab some berries for dinner?"

I gladly accepted her request and grabbed the berry basket and headed out to the bushes. I skipped all the way to them, which were right by Reuben's house, something I was quite thankful for. I needed his advice.

When I got there, it didn't take me long to pick the berries we needed. So, I ran to Reuben's house and knocked on the door.

Amelia answered.

"Hi, who are you here for?" she asked.

"Reuben."

"Where are you going?" she asked.

"Just to the bushes," I said, pointing to them.

"Can I come, too?" she asked.

"Maybe later. Now, are you going to get Reuben?"

Amelia shut the door.

In less than a minute, Reuben was following me to the bushes. "Hi, I must sneak out, okay?"

"What?! No! Why would you do that?" he asked, talking so fast, I could barely keep up with him.

"I have to go to the opening, and this is the only way I can," I said, thinking it was pretty obvious.

"Well, it's a bad idea!" he snapped.

"Look, you're not the boss of me," I said, being snotty.

"And yet, it feels like I always have to keep you from getting into more trouble. You know what? It's not my job to make sure you don't get in trouble," Reuben said, raising his voice, louder than he had ever spoken to me before.

"Then why do you?" I asked, raising my voice back at him.

Reuben sighed. "I don't want to, but it feels like I have to," he said, his voice so soft I could barely hear him.

"You don't have to. That's not your job," I hung my head and made designs in the dirt with my boots.

"I know. I'm sorry. I was getting in your business, and I know I shouldn't do that," he said. "It's just I don't want any of my friends to get into trouble."

"It's okay. You know, maybe I shouldn't sneak out," I said, realizing that if I didn't, I'd miss the trail opening.

"Epateen, maybe you should talk to your mama about this," Reuben suggested with a half-hearted smile.

"My mama won't let me go. She's still pretty upset about what happened at school."

"What happened at school?" he asked.

I always forgot that Reuben went to a different school than Hirram and me.

"I'll touch on that later, but the point is, she won't let me go."

"That is a shame. I sure wish you could. Unless …"

"What?! Reuben … what are you thinking?"

"You could … just maybe … it's just an idea on what you could … or could not … do," he stammered.

"I want to go, so tell me!" I exclaimed, hardly able to stand still until he spilled the beans of his plan.

"You could sneak out ... maybe they won't even know you're gone ... if they're busy doing other things," he said.

"But you told me not to sneak out," I said, beyond confused.

"It's not my business what excuse you make up ... or if you even have to make up one ... it's just an idea," he said.

I thought about it ... for barely a second. "Okay, I'm in! Maybe I won't need to tell them anything!"

Maya Gideon

CHAPTER 14
THE DAY OF THE TRAGEDY

The next morning, I woke up early. It was Sunday, so we had church. My mama usually got me up at 8 a.m. Sunday School started at 9. But I was up by 7:00. I walked down the stairs, where Mama was having oatmeal.

She saw me and her one eyebrow raised. "Why are you up so early? You're not exactly an early bird."

I shrugged.

"You, okay?" she asked.

I sighed and said, "Yeah, I just woke myself up."

I lied. I woke up early because I was so excited about the trail ride.

"Well, there's oatmeal and coffee, not sure you'll want the latter," she said.

"I'll take the oatmeal. Boy, I am hungry," I said.

Mama smiled as she took a sip of coffee.

"I mean, I am thirsty too. Just not for coffee," I said, smiling.

Mama giggled. "I can't understand why you don't like coffee."

"Mama!"

"Okay ... okay ... I'll stop," she said, not about too, though, because she loved to tease me about coffee ... a lot.

"I don't get why you like that dirt," I said, continuing our little joke.

Mama rolled her eyes. "You better not have just called my coffee dirt."

"Or what?" I asked, challenging her.

"Or I'll make you drink it!" She laughed.

I sighed and rolled my eyes. I knew I had to stop teasing her, but I didn't want to. It had been so long since I joked with her.

"Well, do you have orange juice?" I asked.

"No, sorry. But we have milk. Your papa milked Darsey an hour ago," she said.

Darsey was our dairy cow.

"Okay, I'll have some milk. Can you get my oatmeal?" I asked.

In less than five minutes, I was sitting at the table eating oatmeal with a cup of milk.

Hymnal Song #4 – Love is Everything:

One ... day, one day, we will find a savior, one day, that day ... will be glorious. We will, we will, we will, worship that savior, that day, we will worship. That day ... we will worship. Worship. Worship. Then a word came, one stronger than anything ... the word ... Love. Love, Love is great, more powerful than anything. That savior, gave of that. That savoir, gave of Love. Love is everything. Love is everything ... everything, that is what love is.

The Hope of Epateen

I read the song's lyrics as I sang.

We were at church, wrapping it up with the final song.

"Good song, now let's talk about that savoir who gave us love, does anyone know his name?" Pastor Carkoeir asked.

At that moment, I stopped listening, and thought about the ride I was about to go on. I was so excited!

It was 1:00, and in two hours I would go on the ride of all rides! I would sneak out. And go on that wonderful ride!

My mama walked up the stairs. "Hey, look what I found ... it's your old stuff!"

She set the box on the table in my room then went back down the stairs.

I opened the box, and I found my old diary. The last entry was a week before the fire. I had written only three entries about my new life in my new diary.

But, by then, it was 3:00. Time for action!

Mama was going to the market, and she would be gone for a while. Papa had a field he needed to work. So, I saddled up Tango and rode to Duke's Trail.

Seeing Reuben and Hirram, I waved to them. "Hi, you ready?"

They nodded.

I saw the bumpy dirt trail surrounded by green leaves and lots of trees ahead of us.

"Okay, all, let's ride!" the trail guide hollered.

We rode to a steep hill where a tree's roots were hanging out where you could see them. We went just a little bit down that hill, as the trail guide told us not to go too much further.

When we got closer, I saw a very dirty river racing at rapid speeds.

"Whoa! Look at that!" Reuben said.

Everyone came just a little further down the steep hill. We were all amazed.

But the amazement didn't last long. Something happened in the blink of an eye … an avalanche!

Next thing I knew, I was hanging onto a root, along with everyone else.

My root was sturdy, and I had a good grip. I looked down, the cold water was rushing fast. If you fell in, you wouldn't come out alive.

I saw a little boy hanging onto a weak root. His face was red. He only looked to be about 7.

Then … I saw him lose his grip, and he fell into the deadly water. He was gone. Just like that. *Gone.*

I was so sad my heart was literally hurting.

That's when I saw Reuben … he also had a weak root, and he didn't have a good grip on it.

No! He wasn't going to fall!

I looked around, but everyone was in trouble. So, I climbed up on top of my root, and I reached the top of the hill, pulling myself up.

I ran to the police office as fast as I could, my lungs burning all the way there.

"Help! Hurry! Get things to help us. Hurry!" I jumbled my words together.

Officer Thicker sprang into action. "Get your things crew! Hurry, hurry!"

Soon, I was leading them to the accident.

When we got there, Reuben's root was starting to break.

Time froze and horror filled my eyes. But when time unfroze, Reuben's root ripped apart, and he fell into the deadly water.

He was gone. *Gone. Forever.*

I froze again, as did everything around me. Then, time started to move once more, but ever so slowly.

I saw people trying to climb up the root they were hanging onto. I saw the police reaching their hands out to help them. I saw the police lower a man with a rope-like thing to grab people and pull them up to safety. I saw Hirram taking a police's hand as he pulled him up to the higher ground, safely.

I saw a lot of things that day … a lot of awful things.

Maya Gideon

CHAPTER 15
THE HERO'S REWARD

"Hon, I know things seem hard, but you're a hero," my mama said.

"I don't feel like one," I replied, unable, no matter what I did, to soothe the sharp pain piercing my heart.

"But you are."

There was a knock on our front door, and Mama answered it.

"It's Mrs. Elker. She has something for you."

I went to the door. I wasn't dressed, and my hair was a mess.

"Yeah?" I managed to grumble.

"I have berries for you. And the town chief has something for you too, you know, because you saved so many people," Mrs. Elker said.

"Thanks. But I didn't save Reuben," I said, my voice cracking.

"You're still a hero," she said and patted my shoulder.

"Yeah, I guess."

She handed me the berries. "Enjoy these. Epateen, you're a strong girl. You'll get through this."

Then, she left.

I turned around and gave Mama the berries. "Mrs. Elker said the town chief has something for me."

"Oh, that's good. Why don't' you run up and get it."
"Naw."
"Okay ... then, I'll go get it for you," Mama said and hurried out the door.

In fifteen minutes or so, she was back and handed me a gold coin. I smiled, rubbing my hands against the cool bumpy surface.
"So, why don't you go see Hirram," Mama said.
"Mama, you should know how awkward that would be," I said, knowing she was right but dreading seeing him for the first time after that horrible day.
"You're his friend ... go see him," Mama demanded.
I sighed, grabbed my coat, and walked out the door.

Knock-knock.
Hirram answered. "Hi ... umm ... hi."
"You want to come over?" I asked.
"No. I gotta help Mama bake an apple pie for Reuben's family."
"Oh. Maybe I can help."
"Ah, no. You're probably really busy," he said.
"Why would I be busy?" I said, having no idea why he would think that.
"You know, you being the hero and all," he said, looking at the floor.
"If I were busy, why would I be knocking on your door?" I asked, tired of the hero stuff.
"Good point," he replied and almost smiled.
He invited me in and showed me toward the kitchen, where his mama was baking. The kitchen had dark brown wood for its walls and its floor. There was an island counter, and a red kitchen mat.
Hirram's mama had blond hair and greenish-bluish eyes. I suddenly realized that it was kind of odd that I had not met her until that moment.
"Hirram, who is this?" she asked.

The Hope of Epateen

"Mama, this is my friend, Epateen Vallez."
His mama turned to me.
She had a nice smile.
"Dear, Epateen. My name is Roadam. It is nice to meet you," she said, wiping her hands on her apron.
"Mama, may we help you bake?" he asked.
"Please do!"
We baked for a while until finally, the pie was done.
And that meant it was then time for an even more awkward moment, delivering the pie to Reuben's family.

Knock-knock.
Hirram knocked on the door.
Elvira answered.
"Wut?" he asked, his tiny eyes wet as if he'd been crying.
"Can we see your mama?" Hirram asked.
"Uh ... no. I get Sissy," he said and shut the door.
It soon opened again, and there was Amelia.
"Hi," she said, her voice heavy and sad.
"Can we see – "
Amelia cut me off.
"Reuben? Well … well, you can't see him anymore," she said, blinking her eyes over and over again, as if she were trying to keep giant tears away.
"No. Not Reuben. Can we see your mama?" I asked, lowering my head.
"Oh. I'll go get her," she said and shut the door once more.
We waited a little bit. When the door opened again, it was Reuben's mama.
"Here, Ma'am. We're so sorry about Reuben," Hirram said, his voice shaking.
"Oh, thank you. Did you both make this?" she asked.
"Yeah, we did," I replied.

"Oh, you two are just so sweet! Reuben loved that you were his friends. He said that you were the best friends he'd ever had. Thank you for being so nice to him. And thank you for this pie," she said, sounding sad and happy at the same time.

"Of course … and we are sorry about Reuben. It must be really hard for you. I know it is for me," I said, really not knowing what to say but trying my best to make us all feel better.

"Thank you. And yes, it has been hard, but we're all starting to get around okay without him. Although, I know I will cry every day for a while," she said.

We talked to her a little longer before heading back to our homes.

It was Monday, and our teacher had decided to call off school until Wednesday. Her nephew was also on that terrible trail ride.

When I got home, I told Mama about the last several hours at Hirram's and then at Reuben's. Then, I decided to write in my diary. It really helped. I wrote what I felt. I also did some doodling. I left this world and went into mine, where I was able to forget all about how hard it had been lately.

Soon, it was dinnertime. We had chicken.

After we finished eating, I went to my room, and that's when I heard Mama and Papa talking about the battles and about gold stars.

CHAPTER 16
GOLD STARS

The next morning, Talkie woke me up with a bunch of kisses.

Looking out my window, I saw a beautiful sky, and the sun was shining.

I walked downstairs. Mama already had breakfast on the table.

Maybe Sunday and Monday were just a bad dream, I thought.

I ate all my food and got ready to go to town as Mama had asked me to go buy some supplies.

It was already October, and the air was cool. I felt a slight chill as I walked into the supply shop.

I looked at the list Mama gave me and bought the items she had asked me to. Then, I headed home.

"Is it Sunday?" I asked, handing Mama the things I bought.

"Nope, it's a beautiful Tuesday morning, Epateen."

That's when I knew for sure that none of this was a dream.

Mama looked at me, and she was smiling. "Epateen, we have a surprise for you."

"What?" I asked, trying so hard to focus on what she was saying, but not having much luck.

"It should arrive any minute now."

I sat down at the table with a paper and pen and started to draw a horse-like figure.

I heard the door open, and when I turned around, I couldn't believe it!

There was my brother Nolan! He was home from fighting in the war!

I smiled as I ran and hugged him.

The year was 1916, so I hadn't seen him for two whole years!

"Nolan! You're here! Why?! How?!" I asked.

"Hi, Lil' Munkey. M.U.N.K.E.Y is how it's spelled, in case you forgot," he teased.

"I didn't forget! How could I?! For a while, you were the only thing on my mind. I missed you," I said, smiling up at him.

"I know, Munkey. And I missed you. I heard things haven't been easy for you either," he said.

"You wouldn't be wrong. Wait. Did you say *either*? Which means you've had struggles too," I said.

Nolan laughed.

That laugh where his face still looked like everything was fine, which was my second favorite part about him.

"I've been fighting in the war, Munkey!"

He said it loud but not as if he were mad at me, rather just to emphasize that in wartime there were lots of struggles.

"For instance, my friend Alex, well … he left us for his gold star," Nolan added, his voice suddenly very soft and sad.

"What's a gold star? Is it some reward? Is it some upgrade in the army?" I wondered out loud.

"Sadly, no, Munkey … when a son is killed in a war battle, their parents get a gold star to hang in their window, as a memorial for the boy, or man," he explained, his voice heavy.

"So, Alex having a gold star means that he's dead?" I asked.

"I hate to say it, but yes."

I looked at our window, imagining a gold star hanging there.

No! There would be no gold star in our window. Nolan would be just fine. Papa walked downstairs and spotted Nolan.

"Nol! My boy! My son! My very brave son! It's *You*! You're here! Oh, Nol, it is good to see ya again!" Papa exclaimed, giving Nolan a huge hug.

Talkie ran to Nolan and greeted him with lots of wet kisses.

"Talkie! Hey, doggie. You're a house dog now. Good for you," Nolan said, patting Talkie.

"Yep, he's a house dog," I said.

Nolan turned to me and smiled. "Alright, Munkey, show me around your new stomping grounds."

Maya Gideon

CHAPTER 17
WELCOME THE GUEST

The next day was great, especially because Nolan told us he would be staying for three whole days.

The first thing we did was go on a trail. We went on Barnial's Tifferbitt Trail.

I forgot about Reuben (and Hirram) ... all I could do was be happy Nolan was with me, and I was determined to show him everything!

"Nolan, look! It's Barnialess Waterfall," I said, pointing at the beautiful waterfall with mossy rocks covered in slippery wet waves.

There was a pond at the bottom of the waterfall, which gave us a great place to rest a bit.

"Yes, it is nice. In the war, I have traveled throughout the world. I have seen many waterfalls that this one doesn't compare to."

"Wow! Too bad I have nothing like that to *wow* at ... just this small thing of beauty," I said and giggled.

Nolan shared a laugh with me, which was another one of my favorite things to do with him.

A while later, we headed home, and along the way, I showed him Reuben's berry bush. It now had blueberries on it, and they looked fresh and ready for picking.

"Oh, nice. Although, I have seen many better berry bushes out in the world, like-"

"Nolan, I'm glad you're back from the war, but these berries taste great, so try one," I said, thinking that even though I hadn't been out in the big world yet, like he had, I still knew a great-tasting berry when I came across one.

"Ha! Well, would these berries' owners like that?" Nolan asked.

"Well, no, maybe not, but this once belonged to a boy ... he was around my age. And he won't care any longer. He won't," I said, blinking back tears.

"You sure?" Nolan asked.

"Yes," I said, picking a few berries for me and several for Nolan.

Nolan and I ate our berries and went home.

The next day, I told Nolan about Reuben, then showed him around town.

For the most part, he seemed normal, like the Nolan I knew before the war. But there were times where he just wasn't himself. It was almost like he was remembering something really bad, something bad about the war, but he never talked about it.

We had dinner late that night. Then, I went to bed.

The next day was his last day with us.

He promised to write letters.

As a family, we played board games, outside games, and even trivia.

We had a special dinner that night, roasted chicken.

After dinner, it was time for bed.

That night, I dreamed we were in our old town. Sophi was there. Mama was there, and so was Nolan, and me and my papa. Sophi was having dinner with us. I dreamed about her making funny jokes that made everyone at the table laugh. I remember how much Sophi liked to talk, and how Mama would ask her questions, even though she already knew the answers. I remember how she would ask Nolan about school, and how he would always confuse her with his level of math. In the dream, there was no war, and we were all together, and nothing could change that.

But, in the morning, I woke up, and I knew that it was just a dream. Nolan was going back to fighting in the war.

Maya Gideon

CHAPTER 18
IN A BLACK DRESS

It was now mid-November, and Nolan had gone back to fight in the war.

We had been getting letters from him every week.

This particular day was going to be a really hard day for me. It was Reuben's birthday ... and also ... his funeral.

I ate breakfast and then we went shopping and flower-picking.

Before I knew it, it was 1:00.

Wearing my black dress, we walked into the house of Reuben's parents.

I put the flowers we had picked on the stand where Reuben's photo was placed.

Everyone talked and talked.

Then, at 1:30, we headed out to Reuben's rock. It had his name, birthday, the day he died, and a quote.

Mr. Blasser spoke:

Maya Gideon

"Listen … if you are here, you knew this little boy. He was just a little boy. He was smart. Brave. A confident boy. He was amazing, cheerful, and friendly. Now, he may have been just a little boy, but he was big in our hearts. And he had a big heart. As most of you know, today he would have been 13 …"

I stopped listening and looked at Hirram. He looked so sad. And I was sad too.

I looked around … everyone was sad.

I began to cry … and it felt as if I were never going to stop.

CHAPTER 19
DECEMBER SNOW

It was late December, and I got some good presents. Then, on the 29th, we got a foot of snow.

Me and Hirram ran outside, and we had a snowball fight.

"Ha, just give up Epateen," he shouted.

"Oh no!" I yelled back at him, throwing a snowball right at him.

"I will win 'cause I am a snowball king," he said, making another snowball.

"Hirram, you are going down," I said while packing my next one.

We both threw our snowballs and continued to do so for something like an hour.

At the end of the game, I realized Hirram had won.

"Yes, I am the snowball king!"

"Well, I let you win," I said.

And we laughed.

Then, we made snow angels. We competed to see who had the cleanest snow angel. I won that one. After that, we just made them for fun. We also built a snowman, which took forever. But when we were done, it looked great!

Maya Gideon

Mama called me in for dinner.
It was such a fun day.

CHAPTER 20
THE NEW YEAR

The new year came quicker than a bee races to honey. And the new year was 1917. I hoped it would be the year that the war ended.

We were out of school for a week.

We got a letter from Nolan on Sunday. It was pretty boring, which, believe it or not, was a good thing. It meant that he was still doing well.

Later that day (although, it might have been on Monday ... I'm not sure), I hung out with Hirram. We baked a strawberry pie, which did not turn out good. Why? Because we put it in the oven and then lost track of time. (Bet you can guess what happened next ...) When we pulled it out of the oven, it was completely burnt, as in not even edible ... that's how burnt it was.

On Wednesday, my papa and I went on a trail ride. And later that day, I went to the library and checked out a book, which I read five chapters of and then decided to sketch in my notebook. I was now on page 45, but I wasn't worried because it had a lot of pages.

After I drew for a bit, I helped Mama make dinner and set the table.

After dinner, I wrote in my diary then got in my night clothes and read my book.

I blew out my candle in one puff. Then ... I went to bed.

Thursday was boring. I just sat around (in my night clothes), read some of my book, sketched, and wrote in my diary.

Friday, I hung out with Hirram, who told me that for, the last few days, his grandparents had been at his house. We tried to make another pie. But this time, we underbaked it. So, we were gonna put it back in the oven to bake for a bit longer, but Hirram dropped it on the floor.

Saturday, I went to visit Reuben's grave, and let's just say that it was emotional for me.
Then, I went to Hirram's house. Once again, we tried to bake a pie. And you'll never believe it, but it came out perfect! Until ... Hirram's dog, Guwachi, jumped on me while I was holding it, fresh out of the oven. I lost my balance and dropped it. So, pie attempt #3 was also a fail.

On Sunday, we went to church and then went to lunch with some friends from church.
When I got home, I read my book, then went to Hirram's house to see if he could hang out, but he wasn't home. I think he was out for lunch with his family. So, I went home and read more of my book. I also wrote in my diary.
We had dinner, and I went to bed.

CHAPTER 21
THE BEAST OF FEBRUARY COMES

February came. And it was a beast, a very cold one, at that.

At school, me and Hirram had to hang out inside, which was really boring.

I hadn't written in my diary for almost a month.

One day, I went to check on Reuben's berries, and when I saw them, something inside me clicked. I still missed him, so don't take it the wrong way, but I didn't miss him as much ... I had moved on. I knew everything would be okay.

I looked at his berry bush. It was dead. There was no Reuben and no berry bush.

I walked back to my house.

That was all that was exciting for February of that year. Well ... not all of it, I guess ...

We got another letter from Nolan. I read it in bed beside my burning candle:

Maya Gideon

Dear Family

The battles have been rough, especially because the German U-boat has raised its head again. Why can't this war end? It's been on for 3 years now. I know we recently saw each other, but that won't stop me from missing you. A friend of mine in the Army, David, says:

"The war is at its peak of death. The war is bound soon to be over. Done with. A thing for the past. A scare in history forever. The soldiers that fought (us) will remember this in a nightmare. The sounds of fireworks will remind them of gun shouts, bullets racing across the battlefield, not knowing if they're coming straight toward them or not, not knowing if it were their last moments to live. The sounds of crying men being stabbed or being hit by a bullet. Them in pain as they suffer their last moments. The ones who live, like I said, will remember this as a nightmare. But remember, the war is 'bout at end. Victory isn't far. Even if the German's U-boat raises stronger than before, we raise stronger than any enemy. Remember what we are fighting for, our loved ones' happiness. Now, we best reach victory. We will reach victory as long as you remember this: We are strong, and the war will soon be over! Now, men, get to work."

That's what Davis says. I hope he's right about the war being over soon. That was his pep talk to us.

You know, maybe I can come visit again. It's dangerous being on battlefields, but that doesn't stop me from fighting

The Hope of Epateen

for this victory. Hopefully, David is right, and I will see you all soon.

From Nolan

I got done reading his letter. And I hoped David was right too. I was ready for this war to be over.

Maya Gideon

CHAPTER 22
MARCH AND HIRRAM'S BIRTHDAY

March meant it would be Spring soon. Also, it would be Hirram's birthday. He would be 13.

I had an idea what to get him. So, one day, I went to the baking store and saw Mr. Belomtele, the shop owner. I asked him where I could find the ingredients for pie. He had all but one item ... the berries.

I wondered if maybe there were a few survivors on Reuben's berry bush.

I bought the items Mr. Belomtele had then headed to the bush. When I got there, it looked like it was all dead, but I looked deeper. I found one single berry. *That won't work,* I muttered to myself. But I picked it anyway.

I remembered that Mrs. Elker had a berry bush, so I headed for her house.

I knocked on her door.

"Epateen," she said upon opening the door. "Deary, it's been months since I've seen you. At the funeral."

"Yeah. Nice to see you again, Mrs. Elker," I said, hoping she wasn't going to remind me of that horrible day.

"Yes, hon. You are doing better?" she asked and smiled.

"Yes. Much. Hirram is fine too," I said, glad for the positive talk.

"Good. Now, Hero Epateen, what do need?" she asked.

"I am a hero ... I am," I mumbled, knowing the faster I agreed, the faster we'd be onto another topic and hopefully to the reason for my visit.

"Yes! I am glad you finally think so."

"Yeah. Anyway, can I have some berries?" I asked.

"Oh, why that's fine, just tell me what you need 'em for."

I could've told her that it was Hirram's birthday, because we were friends, but I didn't. I lied. I didn't think we were as close anymore.

"We want to bake some pies. You know, me and Mama."

"Yes, go on back now, and pick the finest ones you want."

So, I did.

And they were the finest berries in all of town.

I picked a few more, then thanked Mrs. Elker, and headed home.

Later that afternoon, I was walking to Hirram's house with his gift. I was excited to give it to him.

I arrived at his house and heard him and another girl laughing. The girl had brown hair and dark eyes.

"Hi. I'm here to see Hirram," I said.

"Oh. I … I didn't know that, w-well, that you were-w-were c-coming," Hirram sputtered out.

"Oh, so, Hirram, you're saying that she wasn't invited? But she came anyway? Is that because she is rude?" the girl asked with her hands on her hips.

She said *rude* louder than the other words, which made me a little mad.

"Well, I didn't invite her, I guess," Hirram mumbled and shrugged his shoulders.

The Hope of Epateen

"I thought, because we were friends, I didn't need an invite," I said as nicely as I could muster.

The girl giggled.

"Is that because you're too 'good' for invites? Too important? Think you're better than everyone else?" the snotty girl said.

"No!" I snapped.

"Calm down, Epateen," Hirram said.

"Epateen?" the girl said, and not in a pleasant tone.

"Yeah, her name is Epateen," Hirram said with a challenging edge to his voice.

"Okay. Well, I'm Jessica. The straight A-student. The star student! The shining star! The jewel student! The Best student!"

"Ya think you're better than everyone else?" I asked, and this time it was my turn to have an edge and challenge in the way I spoke.

Jessica rolled her eyes. "You can stop."

"Stop what?" I said, not caring at all how rude I sounded.

"Stop being a mean, rude, jerk to me. Not cool. I don't know why Hirram was friends with you, but at least he saw his mistake and stopped being friends with you."

I turned to Hirram.

"Ep-"

He was cut off.

"Yeah, Ep, just go. He doesn't want you here," Jessica said, turning her nose up into the air as if there was something up there really high that she wanted to smell.

"Wh-" I began.

But then, I was cut off too!

"Beat it!" She was pointing at the road.

"Wait, let me talk-"

Once again, I was cut off.

"Leave! Us! Alone! You weren't invited! So Beat It!"

"Jess-" Hirram attempted.

"You are annoying! And rude-"

(That was Jessica ... cutting us off, again.)

"Jess ..."
(And that was Hirram with one last try.)
"Just shut up and leave us alone, Epateen. We don't like you!"
"Jess!" Hirram screeched. "Leave her alone! She is one of my friends! Don't be mean."
Jessica sighed. "I'm going inside."
She headed away from the door.
"Jess," Hirram said.
"What?!"
"You can say you're sorry."
"I don't have to," she said and kept on walking.
"I'm sorry, Epateen, but she is a great friend," Hirram said so softy he could hardly be heard.
"I can tell."
"Epateen, just try to be friends with her."
"Alright. I'll try. But only because you're asking me to."

There were about ten people inside around Hirram, watching him open gifts.
"Oh. This one is from my cousin, Delores. Thank you, Delores, for ..." He opened the gift. "Oh. A pillowcase. Thank you."
He picked up the next gift. "This is from Jessica! Let's see what it is."
Jessica sat up tall and had a large grin.
It was a model car. It was shiny and black, and the wheels moved.
Hirram's face lit up. "A model car! This is the new version! Thank You! Thank you! I love it!"
He started sharing lots of facts about cars. Turns out, he knew a lot about them. He was really into them.
"Thank you so much, Jessica! You're the best of friends," he said, picking up the next gift.
It was a white blanket from his Aunt Deana.
"Thank you, Aunt Deana."

The Hope of Epateen

Then, he grabbed the next gift. It was a shirt from his cousin Daniele. After that was a pair of socks from his uncle. Then ... he picked up my gift.
He opened it.
At first, he frowned.
Jessica looked happy with that.
Then, he looked at me and gave me a fake smile. "Ahh. T-th-thanks, Epateen. Thank you."
He picked up the next gift.
Jessica looked at me and whispered in my ear, "He hates your gift. But he loves mine. Tip. Actually try when getting others gifts."
I didn't say anything. And lucky for me (and her), she moved away from where I was sitting.
Her words kept repeating inside my head: *Hirram hates your gift. But he loves mine. Hirram hates your gift.*
Hirram hates my gift.
Hirram hates my gift.
Hirram hates my gift.
But he loves Jessica's.
He loves Jessica's.
The party went on, and I stayed until the end. I simply moved on in my mind and tried to enjoy myself.
Jessica didn't talk to me for the rest of the party, which was fine with me.

When I got home, I wrote down what happened in my diary. I said some nasty stuff about Jessica. And honestly, I'm not sorry for calling her a slug and a pile of dirt, or a bug-eyed monster, or a spiked caterpillar that almost everyone wants to step on, or a three-footed unlucky rabbit. That's what I called her in my diary.
Jessica was mean. Rude. A beast.
And why was she mean to me? I don't even know!

But I did know Hirram was my friend, and he wanted me to be friends with her … so, I would try.

That's all I could do … try.

Jessica might be mean, but I was gonna try to be nice to her.

But I was gonna have to try hard. *Really hard.*

Maybe, just maybe, though, we could all be friends. Maybe things could be good.

The three of us could become friends.

Hard to imagine being friends with her, but it was possible, I supposed.

I was hopeful that the three of us would become friends.

I thought we could be.

Yeah, that's what I thought.

I was gonna be nice to her … so, no more snapping at her or calling her names out loud or in my head. Or … I guess not in my diary either. We were going to be friends.

CHAPTER 23
NEW BEGINNINGS

Easter came soon.
My family put on our nicest outfits and went to church.
I saw Mrs. Elker, Hirram, and guess who was with him?
You guessed it ... Jessica.
I sat in the row in front of her. I don't know why my papa picked that row.
"Hi," Roadam, Hirram's mom, said to my mama.
"Why, hello, Roadam. Nice to see you and Hirram. Now, who is this girl?" Mama replied with the sweetest smile on her face.
"Umm, well, it is ... she's ... umm ...," Roadam began.
"Her name is Jessica, Mama," I jumped in, not sure why Hirram's mama just wouldn't say so.
"Jessica, okay," Mama said and smiled at her.
"Ma'am, what is your name?" Jessica asked.
"Why, aren't you so polite. Epateen, if I were you, I would be taking notes," Mama said.
I growled.
"Ha! I see why you say that, Ma'am," Jessica said.

Luckily, the service started.

After it was done, I had to walk with Jessica and Hirram back toward our houses.

On the way there, Hirram's mama had to stop and get groceries. So, we had even more time to talk.

"Jessica, do you have a family or do you just stay with Hirram 24/7?" I asked.

"Oh, umm, well ... I don't really talk about it, and well-"

"It doesn't matter," Hirram cut her off.

That was certainly the first time I'd ever seen him do something like that. *Odd,* I thought.

"Alright ... so, Jessica, what do you like to do?" I asked.

"Well, I love baking. I'll bake all day. My mother and I used to bake pies, cakes, and other sweet foods too."

"Nice! I love baking too! Do you and your mama still bake a lot?" I asked.

There was silence for a second. And then there was a frown on Jessica's face, and she was looking down at the ground. For a moment, I thought she was going to cry.

"... N-no. No. The answer is ... no," she said, her voice more than a little sad.

"Is everything okay?" I asked.

"I don't want to talk about it," she said.

"Okay. Well, how'd you become friends with Hirram?" I asked, suddenly feeling my heart hurt for her, even though I didn't know why.

"Kinda just happened," Hirram answered for her.

"Okay. That's not a lot of details, but okay," I said, not sure what else to say.

He kicked a rock with his shoe and didn't say another word.

"What's your favorite color?" I asked her, deciding to change the subject.

"Purple. Definitely purple!" Jessica said, her voice much lighter.

"I don't know what mine is," I said.

Jessica smiled at me. "You're not so bad, after all."
"You're not that bad either," I said and smiled back at her.
"Sorry for that day. You know … Hirram's birthday."
"Jessica, it's okay. We're friends now. We're on good terms. That's what matters," I said.
And from that day forward, we were friends.

Maya Gideon

CHAPTER 24
THE GIRL WHO RAN AWAY

May started off with school winding down and a trip to Ireland with my papa and mama. We were going to visit my aunt. It took quite a while to get there, but we finally made it.

My Aunt Domania's husband was fighting in the war. Her son, who was 20 years old at the time, burned his hand over a fire, but lied to the government that it was broken to stay out of the war. That said, he lived on the other side of Ireland, so we didn't see him much.

The inside of Aunt Domania's house was a decent size, but the outside was pretty boring.

It was our second day staying there, and I didn't expect her to wake us all up at 6:00 a.m. But she did, telling us that we were going to her friend's public ranch.

At the ranch, there were cows, chickens, horses, and just about every kind of livestock. I also saw this guy with a long black beard, wearing a cowboy hat, and he had on dusty overalls. He was feeding the chickens.

My Aunt Domania saw him too and pointed at him. Then, she started walking really fast towards him.

"Epateen," she called out, "hurry up. I want to introduce you to someone."

I caught up with her and soon, we were right in front of the man. He looked up from feeding the chickens and greeted my Aunt Domania with a smile. He had been kneeling in the dirt, but now he was up and patting her shoulder.

"Domania!" he exclaimed. "Have you come to get some eggs because I have some ready for you!"

"Oh, I thank you, but I am here to show my niece Epateen around your ranch," she said.

The man looked at me and said, "Why, hello there, I'm Cody Palabo."

"Hi," I said.

"How old are you?" he asked.

"I am thirteen. I will be fourteen this summer."

"Well, that is mighty fine because I have a thirteen-year-old daughter too," he said. "She is in the barn right now if you want to go in and say hi."

I nodded and then ran to the big red barn.

On the barn door, a sign read *employees only*. But I thought it was okay if I walked in since Mr. Palabo said I could. So, I opened the door. It squeaked really loud.

Walking in, I saw pigs and sheep in their pens. Sitting on a hay bale was a girl with black hair. She had a pencil in her hands and was drawing in a notebook.

I slowly approached her.

She glanced up at me and then ran away.

"Wait!" I called after her.

But she did just the opposite and kept on running. Before she was out of sight, however, she looked back at me and hollered, "Employees Only!"

I headed for the door, but before I made it, I heard it squeak again.

It opened, and a little boy walked through.

"Who are you?" he asked.

The Hope of Epateen

He looked to be no older than the age of seven. "Who are you?"

"I asked you first," he replied.

"I'm Epateen," I said. "My Aunt Domania is friends with Cody Palabo."

"Are you an employee?" he asked.

"No," I said. "So, who are you?"

"I'm Esten Palabo," he replied, sticking his chest out a little. "Cody is my dad."

"Okay," I said.

"It's employees only," he said, "so maybe you should go."

"I got permission to be here from your dad," I responded.

"Why?"

"I wanted to say hi to your sister," I said.

"Why? There is nothing special about her. Besides, she hates people," Esten said.

"Where did she go?" I asked, thinking that was pretty sad.

"I don't know, but she is probably around here somewhere."

"Can you give me a tour of this place?" I asked.

"Nope!" he said and walked away.

I looked around the barn for a while. I saw a lot of rats, bugs, horses, and other animals. Then, I found this wooden ladder. It led up to a hay loft.

I started to climb it.

There was lots of hay.

I climbed all the way up.

There were tall stacks everywhere.

At the top of one of the stacks, there was the girl who had run away from me. She was drawing in her notebook again.

"Hi," I said.

She looked at me and again said, "Employees only."

"I've got permission to be here," I told her.

She did not say anything back.

"What is your name?" I asked.

She hesitated for a moment. "Ioney."

"Does your dad own this farm?"
She nodded.
"Are you thirteen?" I asked.
"Yeah."
"Your dad told me about you," I said. "I'm thirteen too!"
"Okay ... is he the one who gave you permission to be here?"
"Yeah," I said.
"Why?"
"Do you know someone named Domania?"
"Yeah, she is friends with my dad. She comes over a lot. My family and I know her pretty well," Ioney said, seeming to relax more.
"She is my aunt."
Ioney smiled. "Oh. Okay. Well then, it's nice to meet you."
"Yeah. Same. Could you give me a tour of the place?" I asked.
"Yeah! Definitely," she replied.
Then, she showed me around the farm.

When we were near the pastures, where they kept horses, cows, and donkeys, we saw Esten.
"Hey, Est," Ioney said.
"Hi. What are you doing with that girl?" he asked.
"She is Domania's niece."
"Oh. Cool. But I already knew that," he said with a smirk.
"Me and Esten have met ... when I was looking for you," I said.
"Oh, okay," Ioney said and continued giving me the grandest of tours.

When we were done, we were back in the hay loft talking about sketching and drawing, as if we were best friends. We were laughing and making jokes. Come to think of it, we weren't just acting like friends. We were friends!

CHAPTER 25
TWO NEW BEST FRIENDS

One week passed and me and Ioney were hanging out practically every day.

Some days, we were at the ranch and other days we were at Aunt Domania's house. When we were at my aunt's house, we would draw together. When we were at the ranch, we would do all sorts of things. Sometimes, we would play with the animals or give tours to visitors; other times, we sketched and talked in the hay loft. One thing we didn't enjoy, that we had to do anyway, was chores.

One day, Ioney came over to Aunt's Domania's house with a great idea ...

We were sitting in the living room. I was in my aunt's red puffy chair. It was the softest chair in the house. Ioney was right across from me in my aunt's dark brown rocking chair.

"Okay, so I was thinking that, maybe we could have a sleepover at the ranch," Ioney said, so excited.

"That's a great idea! We could sleep in the hay loft," I said.

"Yeah. I asked my dad about it. He said it would be fine!"

"Perfect! Hopefully, my aunt and parents will say yes too."

And just like that, we started planning what we would do during our sleepover.

I went to ask my Aunt Domania about it. And she said yes! Then, I asked my mama and papa. They also said yes!

I went back to the living room and told Ioney that the sleepover was official. Then, I grabbed my notebook, and we started writing down ideas:

IDEAS FOR AWESOME RANCH SLEEPOVER
1. SNACKS, SUCH AS APPLE PIE
2. PARTY LIGHTS
3. DRESS UP OUTFITS

"Amazing!" Ioney shouted.

"Yes! Let's go to the general store to get all the items we need," I said.

Ioney nodded.

"Aunt Domania, were going to the general store," I shouted.

"Okay," she replied. "You can use the money on the kitchen table."

I took a little bit of the money, not sure we'd need it all, and we walked about ten minutes to town, where all the stores were, including the general store.

As we walked in the store, there was a cool breeze, which felt wonderful.

"Hello and welcome to my fine and dandy shop. Feel free to look around, and please buy what you want. If you need any assistance, you may always ask me. My name is Kerture Didele. Enjoy your shopping," a cashier practically sang to us.

We walked to the fabric area.

'What color should we get?' I asked.

Ioney shrugged.

"What's your favorite color?" I asked.

The Hope of Epateen

"Purple."

"That's my favorite color, too!"

Ioney smiled.

"Purple it is then?" I asked.

"Yeah."

So, we got a few pieces of purple fabric.

"Do you have dress up outfits at your house?" I asked.

Ioney shook her head. "No, not really."

"That's okay," I said. "We'll make something with this fabric!"

We went up to the cashier and checked out. Next stop was the clothing store.

"Alright, now to the clothing store?" I asked Ioney on our way out of the general store.

She hesitated and stuck her left hand in her left pocket. "I don't have any more money on me."

"That's okay, we'll run to my aunt's house to get some more."

"Ok," Ioney replied, her voice sort of uneasy.

We walked a few steps, and I smiled at her, trying to think of something to cheer her up. "Race you there?"

"You bet!"

We took off as fast as we could to Aunt Domania's house. We ran in the door, grabbed the rest of the money on the kitchen table, and hurried back to town.

Once inside the clothing store, we burst out laughing, eventually stopping so we could look around the store. We saw a whole bunch of dresses, one of which was a bright orange dress with a seaweed green apron and a red bonnet.

"You should get that one!" Ioney pointed to it.

I laughed. "Yeah, right!"

After a while, we finally picked out our outfits. Mine was a long white dress that had light blue and light pink flower designs covering patches of more whiteness. Ioney's was light blue with two gold strands going down it in a wavy pattern. It also had dark blue, green, purple, red, and even a few pink flowers on it.

With all our new dresses, we ran back to Aunt Domania's house.

Not long after, we were playing outside in our dresses, when Ioney slipped and fell in the dirt. Her hands were all dirty, and her new dress was now brown.

Ioney started laughing, and I did too.

"Well, I guess we'll have to wash my dress," she said between giggles.

Eventually, we stopped laughing. But it took a while because we really loved to laugh.

CHAPTER 26
BARN SLEEPOVER

The sleepover was the first weekend in June. At about 4:00 p.m. that day, I thought about how in only two hours I would be at Ioney's ranch. I could hardly wait!

I needed to hurry, though, because I had a list of chores to do at my aunt's house first.

In no time, I got them done and walked over to Ioney's house.

First, we went to the barn and started decorating it with hearts and stars cut from paper. We stuck them to the walls. Next, we went into her house and started making a snack of jam and biscuits. We brought them to the hay loft and set them up on a table.

We also brought the Mancala game. We played eight and a half times, to be exact. I won four times, and Ioney won four times. During the final tie-breaking game, Ioney's papa called us in for dinner, so we didn't get to finish that game. We decided to just both be winners!

We were served stew, and it was delicious. Ioney's mama and papa started asking me lots of questions about myself. With so many questions in a row, it was really chaotic. But after I answered them all, it was quiet again, and I could hear every cricket, every rushing stream, and every animal within five acres of their house, which was so calming and nice.

After dinner, Ioney and I didn't know what to do.

"How about if you give me a tour of your house?" I asked as her parents were cleaning up the table.

"Sure!" she said and started my tour from their front door.

The door was cream with a steel knob. Next to the door, on the side, was a wall with a shelf the color of freshly polished wood. On the right, there was a lounging room with a leather couch and a black rocking chair.

As we kept walking, we came to a staircase on the left-hand side, and on the right-hand side was a grayish blue wall.

"We will go upstairs in this tour, but it will be later," Ioney said.

We continued to walk past the stairs to where the wall ended. There was their living room. It looked just like their lounging room, but it was bigger. The walls were the same grayish blue as the one by the staircase. The floor had a tan carpet. Off to the left was a bathroom with wooden walls and flooring.

"Okay, time for the second part of the tour. Upstairs," Ioney said, her eyes twinkling.

Upstairs was a single hallway. And there were four rooms – two on the left side and two on the right.

"The room closest to us on the left side is my parents' room. The second room on the left side is my room. The first room on the right is my brother's room. The room right behind his is another bathroom."

Ioney decided to show me her room next, and I was very excited to see it.

Right across from her doorway, she had windows. On one side of the windows was a white chest of drawers. On the other side was her bed. Her bed had pink sheets with pink pillows, and it was placed vertically. On the wall right beside the door was her closet. The walls of her room were light green.

"This is my room! What do you think?" she asked me, all smiles.

The Hope of Epateen

"I like it!"

"Me too!"

After the tour, we decided to bake a pie. It was a blackberry pie that would fill the house with a sweet, delightful smell.

Once we put the blackberries into the pie crust, we started to make strips for the top with the leftover dough. The dough was like powdery clay, and it was fun to work with.

We gently placed the strips on top of the pie and placed it in the stove.

While we waited for the pie to be done, we went out to the barn and played with Ioney's rabbit. Its name was Fluffy, and it was a grayish brown color.

After we finished playing with the rabbit, we went back inside the house to see if our pie was ready to come out.

Ioney took the pie out and immediately grabbed a fork and stuck it into the middle of it. Then, she popped a bite into her mouth.

"It's hot!" she shouted and spit it out.

I laughed.

We waited five minutes before we tried another bite.

"This is the best pie I've ever had!" I exclaimed.

"Yeah, it's really good," Ioney agreed.

There was nothing better than blackberry pie, a barn sleepover, and new best friends.

CHAPTER 27
THE LETTER FROM HIRRAM

It was soon the end of June, and every day since the sleepover, Ioney and I hung out.

Several nights, I heard my mama and papa questioning when we would be leaving to go back to England, which made sense because I had read an article about how the British Army were planning a big attack against the Germans at River Somme, in France. Whenever we went around town, we would hear people constantly talking about the upcoming battle.

Later one day, while I was eating dinner, Mama walked in with a tightly sealed envelope.

She handed it to me and said, "It's for you."

I opened it up and saw that it was from Hirram.

I read the letter to myself:

Dear Epateen,

The Hope of Epateen

This summer has been super boring with you gone to Ireland. I've been making pies for the market lately. I've mainly been doing that because I have nothing else to do. The general store has some new owners. They are the Nakoni family. They seem nice. The old owners moved away. I'm sure you remember Jessica, well, she also moved away. Speaking of moving away, my parents told me we are moving. This time we are moving to Sweden, a country away from the war. They say with the war going on things are just too chaotic. I hope you are having a nice time in Ireland.

Sincerely,

Hirram

P.S. We are moving in mid-July

I could hardly breathe. I couldn't believe Hirram was moving.
Also, I couldn't believe he said a family named Nakoni now owned the general store. It made me wonder if it was the same Nakoni family I knew in my original town – Sophi's family. Maybe Sophi was there!
"Whose it from?" Mama asked.
"Hirram," I replied. "He's moving to Sweden."
"Oh really?" Mama questioned, sounding just as surprised as I was. I nodded. "And the Nakoni family owns the general store now."
"The same Nakoni family from Bello-Bard Town?" Mama wondered out loud.
I shrugged. "It could be. And I sure hope so!"

I decided that I was going to write Hirram back. So, I grabbed a piece of paper and a pencil. I put the words *"To Hirram"* at the top.

But after that, my pencil just sat on the paper. I couldn't think of any words to write. *"How is Berry Berry Hill?"* I wrote down on the paper. But almost instantly after I wrote it, I erased it.

I folded up the paper and set it to the side. I decided I would think about what to write to him later. Then, I continued to eat my dinner.

For the next two days, I pondered what I was going to write to Hirram.

I just sat in my aunt's soft chair, with a dark brown clip board and a basically blank paper clipped onto it with the words *"To Hirram"*.

I waved the pencil in my hand in front of me.

Aunt Domania sat in a chair beside mine reading a book. "Is everything alright, Epateen?"

I stopped waving my pencil and said, "My friend at Berry Berry Hill wrote a letter to me. I just don't know what to write him back."

"And you said that he is your friend?" she asked.

I nodded.

"Well, then write what you would have said if you were there. Say what you would have said if you were at Berry Berry Hill, and he told you his news, in person. Write the words you would have spoken at that moment," she suggested.

"Don't get me wrong, Aunt Domania, those are smart and wise words of advice, but I need these words to be perfect. It's not as simple as writing down words. Every time I put words on the paper, it just doesn't feel like the right ones. And I don't think the words I would have said at the moment my friend told me the information in his letter would have been right either. I need to find the perfect response, the perfect words, the perfect sentence. It kind of feels like those words don't exist. But they have to, don't they? At least I think they do," I said, beginning to wonder if they actually did exist.

The Hope of Epateen

"There are things that can't be described, my dear Epateen, and there are things that can't be explained. There are feelings that can't be put into words, so there would be no reason for you to not believe that words themselves cannot always describe and explain what we want them to, even if we put them down on paper," my aunt said in her soft, sweet and so very wise voice.

I thought about what she said.

Then, I suddenly knew what to write. The words started spilling out. My pencil raced to finish each letter, each word, and each sentence, cleanly and correctly.

In what felt like no time at all, I finished.

I read it over and over again, making sure the words were the perfect words ... and they actually were.

I held the letter in my hands and read one more time before mailing it:

To Hirram

I read your letter, and when I finished, I couldn't breathe. I didn't know what to think. It was a lot for me all at once. That was why it was so hard for me to write this letter back to you. There were words I was thinking of that weren't words at all. I know that probably doesn't make much sense, but it's true. Anyway, you're moving to Sweden. You're moving in just a few weeks too. My family isn't coming back until the end of the summer. That means you're going to be in Sweden when we come back. So, I won't see you for a long while, but I hope we will be able to write to each other. Honestly, I don't know what I'm going to do without you. You were one of my bestest friends. Speaking of friends, you mentioned about a Nakoni family owning the general store. Back in Bello-Bard Town I had a friend. Sophi Nakoni was her name. So, I was just wondering if they have two kids, one daughter and one son. The girl would be about my age with dark hair. The boy would be a few years younger than her. His name would be Fredderick, and he would have a freckled face. So, if you could get back to me on that, that would be amazing! Now then, you also said that Jessica moved. I am disappointed because I was just getting to know her. She seemed nice, in the end. Well, I'm wondering if her parents took her and moved, because when I talked to her, she didn't seem to want to talk about her family too much. Well, I guess it really doesn't matter. Another thing, I made a new friend. Her name is Ioney. She is very nice and kind. She lives on a public ranch with her family. They own the place and have a fine-sized house just a few acres away from the ranch. That's about all that I wanted to say.

From: Your good friend, Epateen

I finished reading the letter, and I sealed it up in an envelope. I was finally ready to mail it.
"Did you find the right words to say?" my aunt asked.
I nodded. "I think so."
She gave me one of her sweet smiles before going back to her book.

The Hope of Epateen

CHAPTER 28
JULY

It was then the beginning of July. The battle everyone was waiting for had been happening. But we had to wait for detailed information about it.

There was a part of me that had great fear. I wondered if Nolan was in the battle. If he would be okay. And I think Mama and Papa were even more nervous than me. They talked about it almost every night.

So, I decided to push those thoughts out of my head, like I had learned to do so often during that time.

It was dinner time one evening, and Aunt Domania's friends were over. Their names were Mrs. Blacik and Mr. Blacik. They were both in their late 30's, so around my aunt's age.

"Jody, Tom, this is my sister and her husband, along with their daughter," my aunt introduced us.

"It is nice to meet you," Mrs. Blacik said.

"Have you heard about the battle?" Mr. Blacik asked.

The Hope of Epateen

"Why, yes! I believe my husband is fighting in that battle," Aunt Domania said and bowed her head.

"Oh, yes, that's right! Your husband is in the war. You poor thing," Mrs. Blacik replied, her voice full of an anxious sorrow.

"Yes. It has been difficult. I've been writing letters and doing all sorts of things, trying to act like nothing's wrong, but at the end of each day, I worry," my aunt said, tears beginning to fill her eyes.

"It doesn't sound easy, dear Domania. I hope things will be fine," Mrs. Blacik spoke.

"Thank you. My sister is going through the same thing. Their son is in the war," she said, looking at Mama as if she expected her to speak.

"Oh my! That must be rough too," Mrs. Blacik said.

I don't think Mama wanted to talk about it, because she just kept smiling and nodding, without offering a word.

Mrs. Blacik turned to me. "I bet you miss your brother a lot."

I did miss him ... so much.

We had a good bond before he left for the war. And I didn't want that to change. I also wanted to see him again, as it had been such a very long time since the last time he was home.

"Yeah, I do miss him," I answered her softly and nodded.

"War is awful," Mr. Blacik stated.

Everyone nodded.

"Hopefully, this battle will end it," Mrs. Blacik said. "Hopefully."

After that, we started talking about the food and how good it was. And we all seemed to be grateful for the change of topic. I know I sure was.

Then, they asked about my family. They asked about England and Bello-Bard Town. They seemed to be very sorry about what happened there. We also told them about Berry Berry Hill.

After our dinner was over, they left.

My aunt seemed to have nice friends too.

CHAPTER 29
THE NEWS

On July 12th, I went to Ioney's ranch, and she let me ride one of her horses.

I rode Luna, a dapple-grey horse.

Ioney's dad taught me the basics of riding, but Ioney looked way better than I did galloping over the two-and-a-half-foot jump in their outdoor arena.

After that, we went to see the new donkey she had gotten a few days earlier. It was a white donkey with brown spots and blue eyes.

"His name is Spots," she said.

While we were admiring Spots, Esten came up to us. "Can I ride him, please?"

"Of course not," Ioney said.

"Why not?" Esten whined.

"Cause he's my donkey, and I said you can't ride him," Ioney argued.

"Fine!" Esten stomped off.

The Hope of Epateen

After that, Ioney asked me when I would be going back to Berry Berry Hill. I told her I didn't know yet. And I think we were both kind of sad and worried about that.

Later that day, Ioney had dinner with my family. "You know what we should do?
"What?" I asked.
"We should have a sleepover here tonight," she said.
"That sounds like a great idea!"
So, I looked at Aunt Domania and my parents.
"Can we?" I asked.
My aunt smiled and said, "I don't see why not."
So, I gave my parents my prettiest smile, hoping they would say yes.
"Well, since it is your birthday tomorrow, I guess you can," Mama said.
"Come on, Ioney! Let's go and see if your parents are okay with you spending the night!"
We ran as fast as we could to Ioney's house.
After her parents said yes, we stopped by Spots' paddock to say *hi* before heading back to my aunt's house.
We first went into my room.
When she saw it, Ioney's jaw dropped. "Your room is so boring, Epateen! Why it's just a bed with gray walls and a suitcase in the corner."
"Yeah, I've been meaning to decorate it, but I haven't gotten around to it," I said.
"If you want to, we should decorate your room! I have some great ideas," she suggested, with such excitement it would be hard not to agree.
"We could do that, but just remember, this room is temporary. So, the decorations may not be up for too long, depending on when we leave."

"Yeah, but it's never too soon or too late to decorate," she replied with a hopeful smile.

"Alright ... it does sound pretty fun. Even if I have to take it down soon, it'll be worth it."

For the next hour and a half, we crafted and laughed.

And when we were done, it looked amazing!

There was a garland of golden cut-out stars hanging on the top of each of the gray walls. We also brought in some shelves and drawers Aunt Domania had as spares. There were two shelves we painted white. One we put to the left of my bed. The other, we used straight across from my bed. On the shelf near my bed, there was a picture of my family on the right, and on the left, there was a purple glass vase with some lavender in it. On the other, we put a wooden sign that read in cursive: *This Beloved Room.*

There were also white painted drawers into which we transferred all my clothes from my suitcase.

"Wow, it looks fantastic!" Ioney said and clapped her hands.

"Yeah, we did great on it," I agreed, unable to stop smiling.

For the rest of the night, we played different games, including board games and card games with my family. We also did each other's hair.

The next morning was my birthday – my 14th birthday!

First, I woke up Ioney.

She wished me a happy birthday as we walked to the dining room for breakfast.

We had my favorite breakfast – waffles. We ate every last one we received as my family kept wishing me a happy birthday.

After breakfast, I opened my gifts.

My aunt got me a glass sculpture of a dog. Ioney got me a dream catcher. My parents gave me some dresses.

I said my *thank you's* to everyone and then took some time to really admire my gifts.

"We actually have one more gift for you," my parents said.

I looked up at them, more than a little curious.

"We have noticed that you have become quite fond of Ireland and enjoy being here so much. So, we have decided … to let you stay here, after we go back," my parents said it slowly, but also with joy-filled voices.

"Really?!" I said, beyond excited.

My parents both nodded.

"We're going to write you letters, and I hope you will write back to us," my mama said with tears in her eyes.

"Of course, I will," I said.

"I can't believe it! You're staying here!" Ioney said it so loud she was almost shouting.

I turned to my aunt. "You're okay with this?"

"Don't worry, dear, your parents asked me if it was fine. And yes, of course, I am okay with it," she said and gave me her sweet smile.

I looked at my parents. "What about Berry Berry Hill?"

"Whenever you're off school for a bit, we'll have Domania bring you down so you can see us and your friends at Berry Berry Hill. During the summer, we'll come down and stay here for the entire summer," Papa said.

"What about Sophi?" I asked.

"We'll see if it's the same Sophi in Berry Berry Hill, and if it is, we'll let you know, so you can send each other letters," Papa added.

A smile began to form across my face. I could feel it as I hugged my family.

"Thank you," I said.

The rest of the day I spent with Ioney, making all kinds of lists about what all we could do together in Ireland.

CHAPTER 30
THE LETTER IN THE ENVELOPE

When August rolled around, it was about time to start thinking about school. We started to collect my supplies – ink, slates, chalk, crayons, and paper. I was excited to go to Ioney's school.

I went to her house one night, and her family served us dinner. It was meatloaf, corn, and potatoes.

I asked Ioney about the school, the kids, and the teacher. I also told her about what happened to me back at my old school, before we came to Ireland, and about how I liked to draw too much.

She laughed at my story and told me how nice the kids and teacher were at her school, which made me very happy.

Esten began talking about who knows what. He was probably the most talkative kid I had ever heard. Ioney's parents liked to talk too. There was so much talking at their table, I was surprised anyone had time to breathe or eat.

I loved that Ioney's mother was originally from London. She said she moved to Ireland with her family when she was six. Ioney's papa told me he lived in the very same house we were all eating dinner his whole life. Ioney's mama said they sometimes took trips to London to

The Hope of Epateen

see her older sister who moved back there with her husband. She also told me about how they have a pond on the property and, when winter comes, they like to go skating on it.

It was a while before I looked up at the clock, and I couldn't believe it was 9:00 p.m. I politely interrupted one of Ioney's mama's sentences and told her it was time for me to start heading home. So, Ioney's papa walked me home.

When I got home, my parents and aunt were waiting up for me. My parents said I needed to get to sleep because we were having tea with the Benchmen's early the next morning.

"Who are the Benchmen's?" I asked.

My aunt just waved it off and said, "You'll meet them in the morning."

So, I went to bed.

In the morning, at 6 a.m., we were at the Benchmen's house.

Their home was small and cozy. They were older people, looking to be maybe in their early 70's.

They served us tea.

Mrs. Benchman was really interested in me. I felt the presence of her eyes watching me more than once. And it was a little uncomfortable.

"Epateen? Is that your name?" she asked in a soft and calm voice.

I nodded, a little nervous about what she might say next.

"Epateen is a lovely name, one I don't believe I've heard before," she said, smiling while she spoke.

"Yes, we named her after my great aunt, who also played an important role in my life," my mama explained.

Mrs. Benchman nodded, still smiling and looking at me.

"I heard you have a brother, who's a soldier?" Mr. Benchman questioned.

I nodded.

"I heard in an article that that big battle that everybody was hoping would end the war failed," Papa said.

"Yes, I heard that too ... so unfortunate," Mr. Benchman replied in a low voice.

"Epateen, your hair is so unique. Pure blond on the roots but gets into more of a dirty blond as it goes down. The tips of your hair are actually completely brunette," Mrs. Benchman remarked, changing the topic.

I didn't really like that she was changing the topic because now it was back to being about me.

"Epateen is a very smart girl. She will be going to school year-long here in Ireland," Aunt Domania said.

"Lovely! Maybe we'll be able to meet up again," Mrs. Benchman said with an even bigger smile, if that was possible.

I decided I didn't like her.

"Yes, we should do that. But now, we should start heading back to the house, but thank you for having us," my aunt said.

I think she could tell I wanted to leave, and maybe she did too.

So, we said our goodbyes, and we left.

It wasn't long after we got back to my aunt's house that there was a knock on her door.

I didn't realize it then, but that knock on the door would change my life forever.

The knock that was three gentle taps. The knock where everybody in the house stopped and stared at the door, not wanting to answer it. The knock that just felt off, wrong. The knock where we slowly opened the door to find a man wearing an Army suit. The knock where the man gave us a letter and said, *"I'm sorry for your loss"*, before we closed the door.

It was that letter, that piece of paper making our hearts break ...the letter telling us that my brother was dead.

The Hope of Epateen

CHAPTER 31
THE SECRET MEADOW

 I didn't talk to anyone for weeks. In fact, it was early October before I said a word to anyone besides my parents or aunt, except on the rare occasions when I was forced to talk to my new teacher, Mrs. Delhii.
 Ioney's family had brought over a fruit basket and said that they were very sorry for us.
 So, I finally started to talk to Ioney again. She never brought up my brother. She knew not to.
 Even then, I knew I wasn't myself. I certainly didn't feel like myself.
 Nolan's funeral had been the week after we got the letter, but it felt like yesterday.
 I started to hang out with Ioney, every now and then.
 My parents came to the decision to leave for England in early November. They asked me if I wanted to come with them. But I told them no. Berry Berry Hill would remind me of the friends I didn't have ... and the brother I didn't have.
 It took a few more weeks before I started to act like myself again. The days were long and slow. But I eventually began to joke here and there with Ioney. They were simple jokes, and I still felt guilty about

The Hope of Epateen

them sometimes. But my parents said it was good that I was starting to be myself again, especially because it had been two months since that letter came.

There was one day I went over to Ioney's house for dinner. Her parents talked about how soon the pond would freeze over, and we could all go ice skating.

I smiled and nodded. I tried to smile when I could, even though it wasn't easy.

"I'm going to go get something from my room, Epateen, wanna come?" Ioney asked.

I followed her upstairs.

She walked into her room and came out with a book.

I turned to go back downstairs, suddenly noticing that Ioney was staring at a door in the hallway.

In the tour she gave me when I first came to her house, she didn't mention anything about that door. I just thought it was a storage room. But now, she was staring really hard at that door.

"Ioney," I said, trying to get her attention.

"Sorry, it's just that this was once Emmerald's room," she whispered.

At first, I was confused. "What do you mean?"

"Emmerald was my sister. My older sister," she said, her voice still very soft.

"Was?" I wondered out loud.

She nodded. "She was two years older than me. I was only four when she got sick," Ioney said, looking at her feet.

"Oh," I spoke softly.

Ioney looked up at me. "Follow me," she said, grabbing my hand and taking me down the stairs and out the door.

"Where are you going?" her parents called out behind us.

"To the meadow," she answered them.

We walked through the woods behind her house. I thought about the meadow that Ioney told her parents we were going to. I had so many questions.

Soon, we were there.

It was a plain field with a small hill in the distance, and on top of that hill was a singular tree.

We walked to that hill and up to the top of it and sat under the tree. I looked down, and there was nothing but green grass and a wide-open field ... except for one stone in the middle of it.

"Do you see that stone?" Ioney asked.

I nodded.

"That's Emmerald's stone. It's here because she loved this place. I can remember what she called it ... her Secret Meadow."

"Oh," I said, looking all around. *The Secret Meadow,* I thought, knowing how much Nolan would have liked it here too.

The Hope of Epateen

CHAPTER 32
WHEN THE SUN SETS

The sun was beginning to set at the Secret Meadow. And I thought about what had happened over the last couple of years of my life ...

My town was bombed.

I had saved many people from a deadly river ... but not my friend.

I had come to Ireland and made a new best friend.

My friends from Berry Berry Hill moved. But, my old friend Sophi might now be living in Berry Berry Hill.

I lost my brother.

Found out my best friend's secret.

And now, I was sitting here with that best friend, Ioney.

"I used to think that seeing Emmerald's stone down there would make me cry every time I was here. But now, instead of being sad, I am happy. Happy that she was my sister. Because, at the end of the day, it's who's in your heart that matters. The sunset of this place is beautiful, Epateen. It symbolizes the end of the day, and that even though the changes in our lives are big challenges, they're obstacles we can overcome. They let you know to never give up," Ioney said.

The Hope of Epateen

I took a deep breath, and when I looked back up at the sun setting, the past two years flashed before my eyes again.

I closed my eyes and just allowed the memories to pass by me.

Changes had happened … big changes. Changes that brought happiness, excitement, and love. But also changes that brought sadness, loss, and misfortune. But change was also the reason we were who we were. Change was a big part of the world. It's the reason we could bear hardships.

I thought about all that, while Ioney and I remained completely silent.

The evening breeze and the crickets that were starting to come out were the only sounds for miles.

Finally, Ioney said, "We should start heading back, if that's alright?"

I was silent for a moment longer before I answered, "Yeah, we should go. But this sunset is truly amazing. It's so beautiful. It's like watching all my memories in an instant. I would love to come back here sometime and see the colors once again play their melody. It changes every minute in such a gorgeous way. It's perfect. Unlike many things, each change in the colors is absolutely perfect."

We were silent for a moment more before Ioney gave me a mischievous smile and said, "Race you back to my house?"

"It's on! I'll beat you there!" I shouted, returning her ornery smile.

Then, with that, we ran as fast as we could down the small hill and away from the beautiful colors of sunset in the Secret Meadow.

Maya Gideon

EPILOGUE
MAY 1932

I am just now putting down my pen. I have been writing for hours, finishing every last detail of my story.
I flip through each and every page with care.
There are parts of me that are a bit disappointed that I never included in the story above anything about the war's end. But, I do remember it well. It was such a glorious time, with celebrations and parades.
I also didn't include anything about when I saw my childhood friend, Sophi Nakoni, for the first time after many years apart. I was 15 and was visiting Berry Berry Hill in England. I had been staying with my parents for a month before returning to Ireland. Sophi's family did indeed own a shop in the town. It was so nice to see her again.
I also wish I would have mentioned more about my school life. I always had good grades, and after I graduated, I attended college and received my Doctorate degree. I am now a lawyer, who gets paid well and lives in a nice home with my husband.
I have also made many friends over the years, but Ioney and I are still the bestest of friends. She lives only two blocks away from me,

The Hope of Epateen

and we hang out often. She went to college and got her bachelor's degree. She is a 7th grade teacher.

I don't see Aunt Domania as much as I used to. My uncle returned from the war in 1918, but he never was the same. He recently died in February of illness.

Knock-knock.
I rise from my desk, my legs aching from sitting for hours.
I go to the front door and answer it.
It is Ioney and our other friend, Shelby. We met Shelby in high school, and the three of us became great friends. We do lots of fun things together.
I have completely forgotten that we are going to go out for dinner.
I quickly get my stuff, and we start walking to a nearby restaurant.
I tell them about the book that I have just finished.
"Do you plan on publishing it?" Ioney asks.
"I don't know," I say.
"You should publish it! I'd love to read it," Shelby says.
"Well, maybe I will," I respond and shrug my shoulders.
"You've told me that it's about you, but what exactly about you?" Shelby asks.
"It's about my life, and what it was like during the war."
"I know I'll read it," Ioney pipes in.
"Me too," Shelby agrees.
We are at the restaurant now, and we pull open the big wooden doors and walk inside.
"Well," I say, "you'll have to wait for the book to be published first before you can read it."
"You should start editing it today then," Ioney says, and then smiles and winks at me.
"I should?"
"Yeah!" Shelby exclaims. "Hurry up! Get it finished so we can read it!"

I think for a moment and realize what good things publishing my book could do. People will get a perspective on my experience during the war. It will help them know that whatever they are going through, they aren't alone. They can always choose to have Hope.

So, I look at my friends and with a gentle, soft voice, with a hint of excitement I can't contain, I say, "Well, maybe I will publish it."

THE END

NOTE FROM THE AUTHOR

I am Maya Gideon. I have been working hard on this book since 2020. While it is the first book I am publishing, I hope that it is not my last. While writing this book, I have done much research and learned many things. Though writing the book was a long process, it was enjoyable. It is amazing to see how the story went, and how the ideas I originally had were then later scratched to make it perfect. It turned out great!

Thank you for reading!

~~ *Maya*

ABOUT THE AUTHOR

I am Maya Gideon. I started writing this book for fun when I was 10 years old. Now, in 2024, I am in 7th grade. I enjoy school, and ELA is my favorite subject. I live in St. Louis, Missouri with my parents. I do competitive gymnastics and love to hang out with friends and family.

I would like to thank my parents – Debbie and James Gideon – for all the support they've provided.

BOOKS BY THE AUTHOR

Historical Coming of Age Novella

THE HOPE OF EPATEEN

More Coming Soon!

Made in the USA
Monee, IL
22 February 2024

53935913R10079